How to Make
a Fortune
with Other
People's Junk

How to Make a Fortune with Other People's Junk

An Insider's Secrets to Finding and Reselling Hidden Treasures at Garage Sales, Auctions, Estate Sales, Flea Markets, Yard Sales, Antique Shows and eBay

G. G. Carbone

McGraw-Hill

New York   Chicago   San Francisco
Lisbon   London   Madrid   Mexico City   Milan
New Delhi   San Juan   Seoul   Singapore
Sydney   Toronto

The **McGraw·Hill** Companies

1 2 3 4 5 6 7 8 9 0   2DOC/2DOC   0 9 8 7 6 5

ISBN 0-07-144642-7

How to Make a Fortune with Other People's Junk is in no way authorized by, endorsed, or affiliated with eBay or its subsidiaries. All references to eBay and other trademarked properties are used in accordance with the Fair Use Doctrine and are not meant to imply that this book is an eBay product for advertising or other commercial purposes.

Readers should know that garage sales, auctions, online auctions and any other type of sales described in this book have risks. Readers who participate in these activities do so at their own risk. The author and publisher of this book cannot guarantee financial success and therefore disclaim any liability, loss, or risk sustained, either directly or indirectly, as a result of using the information given in this book.

McGraw-Hill books are available at special quantity discounts to use as premiums and sales promotions, or for use in corporate training programs. For more information, please write to the Director of Special Sales, Professional Publishing, McGraw-Hill, Two Penn Plaza, New York, NY 10121-2298. Or contact your local bookstore.

Library of Congress Cataloging-in-Publication Data

Carbone, G. G.
    How to make a fortune with other people's junk : an insider's secrets to finding and reselling hidden treasures at garage sales, auctions, estate sales, flea markets, yard sales, antique shows, and ebay / G.G. Carbone.
        p.   cm.
    Includes index.
    ISBN 0-07-144642-7 (alk. paper)
    1. Secondhand trade.   I. Title.

    HF5482.C37 2005
    658.8'7—dc22   2004026463

*For my parents and mentors, Bob and Barbara Glass,
and for all of you who seek your fortune.
Good luck, and remember, leave no stone unturned
or garage sale empty-handed.*

Contents

Part II: The Basics of Buying

Part III: Making Your Big Profit

Acknowledgments

I feel like I'm writing a thank you for the Academy Awards, where you only have one minute to thank everyone who helped make this moment possible. So everyone, thank you! Thanks to my family (too numerous to list) and my personal and business friends (again too numerous to list). You know who you are because many of you, with your great stories and insider tips, are included in this book. Thanks for the laughs, the photos, and the memories of good times and good fortune. Here's to many more!

Personally, I would like to express my sincere thanks and appreciation to the following people:

Carol Susan Roth, my agent, whose enthusiasm and vision for this book made our quest together a reality.

Donya Dickerson, my editor at McGraw-Hill, who worked with conviction and dedication on this project because she believed in a great idea.

Daina Penikas, senior editing supervisor at McGraw-Hill, her production team, and the marketing and sales team (and others), who together are the heartbeat of this great industry.

Mary M. Ruzicka, of Es Cards Go . . . Ink®, for her fabulous artwork in the book, including the chapter treasure maps, treasure chests, and key icons, as well as her upbeat and positive attitude regarding this adventure.

Wally Lamb, *New York Times* best-selling author and my high school creative writing teacher, who taught me to believe that in due course, all great creative works will come to fruition.

Bob and Barbara Glass, my parents, for their love, encouragement, and wealth of knowledge, as well as their grandparenting skills with my children while I was fervently writing.

Bob Jr., Jeff, and John Glass, my brothers, and their wives, Nancy, Kim, and Kathrina, who also shared their invaluable tips and insider secrets that they acquired on their fortune-hunting journeys.

Laurel Martin, my sister and a published author, who believed in my writing abilities long before I did and told me to "never give up because you have a gift to share with the world."

Byron Martin, my brother-in-law and a successful business entrepreneur, who taught me that great ideas take root and prosper.

Ginger Castle, my sister and a certified gemologist, who showed me that you have to look beyond the surface (to your family) to find a gem that's worth a fortune.

Toby Castle, my brother-in-law and the greatest salesman alive, who told me not to work for him but to "write what you know and love."

Chuck Carbone, my husband and partner, for his phenomenal love and support, and our two sons, Joseph and Benjamin, who let Mommy write her book. Now we can go on that family vacation . . . as long as, wherever we go, we can stop at either a yard sale, antique shop, thrift store, flea market, auction, or all the above. (And you know I'm not kidding!)

Introduction

Saturday, 6 A.M.: You shiver in the cold, early spring morning. The grass is thick with heavy dew. You have a cup of coffee in one hand and a neighborhood map in the other. Your sunglasses diffuse the blinding sunrise creeping over the hill. Your money belt is secured around your waist. An empty tote bag is looped on your shoulder. You adjust your hat and stare at the sign on the garage door that says, "NO EARLY BIRDS!" You repeat your mantra, "The early bird catches the worm, and that's why I'm here."

Of course, you're not the only one waiting for the garage sale to open. Ten other people, probably a few dealers, one or two collectors, and other weekend "junkies" are all here for the thrill of finding a treasure and making a fortune.

> 6:15 A.M.: An elderly woman, let's call her Granny, snaps on her kitchen light and peeks out the window. She's astonished at the size of the crowd. "Henry, the line is almost into the street. You better get the boys up."
>
> 6:30 A.M.: Two young men who look like football players slump into the chairs at the kitchen table. Henry instructs them to keep an eye on the merchandise and to help load any furniture that sells.
>
> 6:45 A.M.: Henry hands the boys a stack of newspapers and a bin of paper and plastic bags. The boys disappear into the garage.
>
> 6:50 A.M.: Granny steps outside and sits down in a straight-back chair. She places a steno pad, a pencil, and a gray cash box on the empty card table in front of her.
>
> 7:00 A.M. sharp: Granny yells, "Okay, Henry, push the button—now."

Your heart beats faster. You shove your empty coffee cup and map into your tote bag. You dig your sneakers into the grass and take a deep breath. A loud humming noise comes from the garage, and slowly, the door opens. You duck under the door into a world of dust-laden artifacts and untold history.

Will you find a treasure today? Maybe. Today could be the day. The garage is overflowing with furniture, tools, china, glass, and books. You quickly scan the tables for something old, new, or unusual and move like a tiger on the hunt to a small, gleaming object on a table in the back corner.

HOOKED ON THE RESALE

If this sounds like you, you are a garage sale, yard sale, tag sale, estate sale, and any-kind-of-sale junkie. Yes, admit it. I am one, too. I'm addicted to the hunt, the deal, and the thrill of buying. Unlike most people, however, I'm also hooked on the resale.

I've been a fortune hunter for the last 20 years. My home is decorated with furniture and accessories that I've purchased at yard sales and auctions. Most of the gifts I buy for family and friends have come from church bazaars, flea markets, or tag sales. Only within the last few years, however, have I turned my passion into a profitable pastime. That's right; I don't keep auction or estate sale treasures anymore. I sell these items for a profit, and I'll show you how to buy and resell other people's junk. It's fun, it's easy, and it's profitable! And if you get hooked on treasure hunting, Chapter 14 tells you how to start your own successful business.

THREE SECRETS TO SUCCESS

Whether you're a first-time buyer or a seasoned pro, I'll reveal tips so that you can make a profit almost immediately with only a small investment of time and money. You'll learn about antiques and collectibles and how to bargain like a pro, you'll experience the thrill of making an awesome buy, and you'll discover essential tips of successful shopping for one reason only—for resale.

My top three secrets to success are

1. *Always buy something unique or unusual, either extra large or extra small in size.* A unique item could turn out to be rare and sought after by collectors. Something unique or unusual isn't necessarily old or antique. Buying barely used or new items at sales and selling them for a profit in a consignment gallery or on eBay is often an overlooked market. Not anymore. The secret is out!
2. *Knowledge unlocks the treasure.* Specialize in a specific collectible area to increase your chances of making a profit on items you buy. Research the market of a particular subject such as World War II military items, 1960s clothing, or Mexican jewelry to give you an edge on the competition when you're buying at a sale. Then learn

about the best places to sell those items whether you sell to another dealer or collector, run the items through a specialty auction, or list them in a specific category on eBay.

3. *The secret to finding the treasure is having fun.* If you don't consider bargain hunting fun, when the alarm rings on Saturday at five A.M., press the snooze button, roll over, and go back to sleep. (And dream about the treasures you could collect while I'm out in the trenches finding them!)

YOU CAN HIT THE JACKPOT!

Can you make extra money buying and selling items you find at flea markets, garage sales, and auctions? You bet! Buy something for $100 and sell it for $200. That's 100 percent profit. You can easily make $100 to $500 in a weekend with little or no risk. Can you make more money, such as $1,000 or more? Sure! You can accomplish this in your spare time, one weekend a month, or every weekend if you get addicted. I'll admit that a fair amount of time and effort is needed, especially if you want to go full time. Or apply the techniques in this book just once to see if you get lucky—and if you get hooked.

Buying and selling are competitive events. Leave the high heels and the silk ties at home. Wear running shoes and deodorant. Put a determined smile on your face. Grab your magnifying glass, flashlight, and map. You're going hunting for a hidden treasure! And to ensure that this adventure is profitable and easy to understand, I've divided this book into three parts:

Part I: Getting Started

As a first-time buyer, this section gives you a quick overview and answers key questions that pertain to garage sales, auctions, and eBay, such as, "What if it rains?" What if they say "No Early Birds?" and "What is an auction with reserve?" Most of these answers are elaborated on in subsequent chapters, so if you want to read about a certain buying or selling technique, you can easily turn to that chapter.

As a treasure hunter, learn the proper gear to wear, what to carry with you, and the items to keep in your car. Get the lowdown on the types of sales, including auctions, eBay, church bazaars, and neighborhood, penny, tag, and yard sales. Whether you're serious about turning pro or staying a weekend warrior, learn how to read between the lines in classified ads to know where to stop first. Then create your own treasure map to target more sales in less time to find the best bargains. Getting to know your community and why you should hook up with the dump attendant or the local hairdresser is revealed. Find out what neighborhoods have the hidden treasures.

Part II: The Basics of Buying

Buying for profit is different from buying to decorate your home or to find gifts for your friends and relatives, and I discuss the basics of buying in this part. However, I want to emphasize that buying for profit is fun, too. In fact, for some people it's a thrill. To add to the thrill, certain techniques emphasized in this part will make you a better bargain shopper. I'll show you how to case a garage sale in under a minute to find the bargains before anyone else does. Role-playing and observation of body language will help you to wheel and deal with sellers. Learn how not only to swim with the competition (dealers and collectors) but also to stay one split second ahead of them. Discover ways to get from the garage into the attic to find those unadvertised, not-for-sale treasures. Reap even bigger profits when you focus on a specialty niche in the marketplace.

Part III: Making Your Big Profit

Once you've purchased all these items, now what? What is junk, and what is truly a treasure? This part shows you how to find out what an item is worth by using price guides, periodicals, and Web sites. You'll learn when to call on experts in the field, such as dealers, collectors, auctioneers, and appraisers. I'll teach you how to sell your goods to the correct marketplace, whether it is eBay, consignment galleries, auctions, antique co-ops or shops, flea markets, shows, or classified advertising. If you're serious about going full time, I'll show you what you need to build a successful business. Finally, success stories and insider tips from others who have bought and sold treasures are also included.

THE AMERICAN DREAM

Remember the old adage that is certainly true, "One man's junk is another man's treasure." We've all heard stories about someone finding the bargain of the century and making a fortune! How about the New Jersey schoolteacher who bought a table for $25 at a yard sale and sold it at a New York auction for $540,000? Or what about the couple that bought a small oil painting for $50 when the auctioneer joked, "This is a Rembrandt," and the painting turned out to be the real thing? Stories such as these keep you hunting for that one item that could land you on Easy Street or Got It Made Boulevard.

I'm on a never-ending treasure hunt, but I can't attend every auction or stop at every garage sale. That's why I'm writing this book. Maybe you'll find that one-in-a-million Picasso painting or platinum brooch with real rubies. And maybe you'll find it because I gave you one extra tip to help you on your quest for the American dream. And remember when you've had a success, no matter how big or small, e-mail me at ggcarbone@earthlink.net.

I sincerely wish you, "Good Luck!" I hope you find a treasure (or two) and make a fortune!

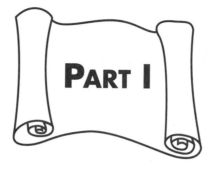

PART I

GETTING STARTED

*(Photo courtesy of Doug and Donna Matteson,
North Kingstown, Rhode Island.)*

1

Unlocking the Doors to Treasures

Welcome to the exciting world of buying and selling. You're about to embark on a fun and adventurous way to make extra money—perhaps even a fortune—if you're in the right place at the right time, get lucky, or use the tools and methods in my book.

The great advantage about going to auctions, garage sales, or any other type of casual sale is that you can make a great buy wherever you live or wherever you travel (even outside the United States). New England has antiques that date back to the 1600s, when some of the towns were founded. You may find a wealth of treasures in that part of the country. California has a rich history but not as old as New England, and hence the merchandise, for the most part, dates from the mid-1900s and later. Of course, exceptions exist, such as when New Englanders move to California and bring all their antiques with them. And the same is true of northerners (or snowbirds) who bring their most valued possessions to Florida.

Different parts of the country use different terms to imply the same type of sale. In New York City, where most people don't have garages, they instead hold stoop sales on the porch or front steps of their brownstone or apartment or even on the sidewalk. In cities such as Minneapolis, people hold citywide garage sales. In California, because of more desirable weather conditions, they have yard sales. In the suburbs on the East Coast, they call them tag sales. Whatever the name, whether it is an estate sale, a porch sale, or a multi-family or neighborhood sale, the principle of buying for profit is the same.

The same holds true for auctions. You can find an auction on every type of tangible and intangible merchandise available. Auctions are held in virtually every state in the country. The Southeast is famous for its tobacco auctions. Parts of the West and some southern states have horse and cattle auctions. Real estate auctions are now prominent everywhere. Personal property auctions consist of estate, antique, consignment, on-site, farm, industrial, general merchandise, storage unit, and household auctions. And within those categories are specialty auctions in every field of interest, including jewelry, books, sports memorabilia, coins, ephemera, toys, clocks, glass, china, furniture, dolls, autos, and boats, to name just a few. An auction occurs virtually every day of the week, 365 days a year. And of course, the most famous online auction, eBay, created a worldwide market for anyone who can access the Internet.

FREQUENTLY ASKED QUESTIONS AND ANSWERS

To start your fortune hunting expedition, you may have some questions you'd like answered first, regardless of how much experience you have. Therefore, let's start by looking at the answers to some of the most frequently asked questions (FAQs). Are you a beginner? I'll show you how to get over your fear of buying the wrong item or not being aggressive enough. Are you a pro? Hopefully, you will glean a few techniques that you haven't tried before. Most of the questions and answers refer you to another chapter in this book so that you can read, in detail, successful tips to get you started immediately. The following questions are organized by topics.

TIP: Fortune doesn't necessarily mean the amount of money you acquire but the results that let you choose your lifestyle.

Get Up and Go

For the best deals, sleeping in on the weekends is not allowed. You must get up for an estate or moving sale between 4:00 and 5:00 A.M. (earlier if you have to travel longer distances). Plan to arrive at a sale by 5:30 or 6:00 A.M. if it's advertised for an 8:00 A.M. start. Are you attending an auction? Arrive as soon as the site opens to preview or inspect the merchandise up for sale. Sometimes the preview is the day before the auction or one to two hours prior to the start time. Are you going to buy on eBay? Relax; you can do that anytime, day or night.

Where Do I Find Out About Auctions and Garage Sales?

Your local newspaper is your best source of sale information. Weekly newspapers have pull-out sections that list all auctions for that week. Garage sales and auctions often are listed in their own category in the classified section of the paper (see Figure 1-1). Specialized antique and auction newspapers, magazines, and journals will list upcoming auctions and estate sales. Other sale

Figure 1-1   Check the classified section of your local newspaper for garage sales, flea markets, yard sales, estate sales, and auction listings.

advertisements are listed on community or church bulletin boards, cable TV, the radio, and the Web. The Resource section in the back of this book has several examples.

What Do I Wear?
If you plan to cruise around to garage sales on a Saturday morning, you will get a workout, so wear a sweat suit, sneakers, sunglasses, and a hat. For an auction, wear comfortable clothing, and dress in layers according to the weather forecast, especially if a sale is held rain or shine. When you're buying on eBay, you can sit in the comfort of your own home and wear your pajamas.

What Do I Bring?
For a garage sale, pack a calculator, a magnet, and address labels in your money belt. Keep blankets, empty boxes, newspapers, and bug spray in your car. For an auction, pack a chair, a blanket, a healthy lunch, and drinks. Other essential equipment including the reasons for carrying a cell phone and a laptop computer are listed in Chapter 2.

What If It Rains?
Some sales will advertise "Rain or Shine." Auctions will list a rain date, if necessary, but otherwise, auctions are held in most kinds of weather, even in

snowstorms in the Midwest. Garage sales are automatically rain or shine. Some yard sale ads don't specify rain or shine or give a rain date, so make a note to attend such sales. The sellers may have the sale inside the house or have an awning or small tarp ready in case of showers.

So Many Sales, So Little Time . . .
Which garage sale or auction do I go to first? The top sales are listed in Chapter 3. Map plotting is essential for garage sales so that you can target more sales in less time. Step by step, with this book, you will learn how to plot your own garage sale treasure map from the newspaper listings. An example of a completed map route is included at the end of Chapter 4. Knowing the people in your community and the best neighborhoods to find hidden treasures is discussed in Chapter 5.

Learning the Lingo

Become familiar with garage sale and auction terms such as *buyer's premium, auction with reserve, as is, where is, white elephant sale, numbers at 7:00 A.M.,* and more. Is a term unclear? Then ask someone. One of the key phrases to learn in this business is *caveat emptor,* which means, "Let the buyer beware."

TIP: Learn to talk the talk, to build confidence and experience to walk the walk. In other words, learn the ropes of buying and selling, and then grab the Tarzan vine, let out the famous yell, and go for it.

Who Is a Dealer?
A *dealer* is in the day-to-day business of buying and selling. Most dealers are registered in the states in which they do business. They have a resale number so that they don't have to pay state sales tax (if any) on their purchases. Many dealers have antique shops. Other dealers buy and sell at shows, flea markets, and auctions, and on eBay. Some of them go to garage sales. Others don't bother. Chapter 8 tells you how to stay ahead of the competition.

What Is a Public Auction?
Usually auctions are open to the public unless they are advertised as something else, such as "by invitation only" (some estate or antique auctions) or "dealer" auction in the case of car auctions. If you're unsure, call and ask. Because of limited space, some auction houses charge a fee that is refundable with a purchase. This ensures that customers who are serious buyers are weeded out from the lookers. When you plan to bring your family, ask what the policy is regarding children. Some auction houses frown on having chil-

dren at a sale where thousands of dollars worth of fragile or rare merchandise is sold.

What Is Auction Fever?

Auction fever occurs when a bidder gets so excited that he gets caught up in the bidding process with the sole intention of winning the bid no matter how high the price goes. Often, when this happens, the buyer spends way over his intended budget and later has *buyer's remorse.*

How Does an Online Auction Work?

eBay, the most well known of the online auction services, is literally open 24/7. If you get the auction bug, you can easily place your bid on one of more than 19 million items offered each day. Figure 1-2 shows eBay's home page. The online procedure to register as a buyer and/or a seller on eBay is an easy step-by-step process. If you make a mistake, you are prompted to reenter your information. To buy or sell, you must give eBay your credit card information. You also can register for a PayPal account (eBay's online payment method). Some sellers also will accept money orders, cash, or checks, but the individual seller sets up payment. eBay has a variety of auction methods, including fixed-price, ascending-price, Dutch, Yankee, reserve price, buy it now, and private auction. Whether you buy or sell on eBay, applicable fees apply on either end.

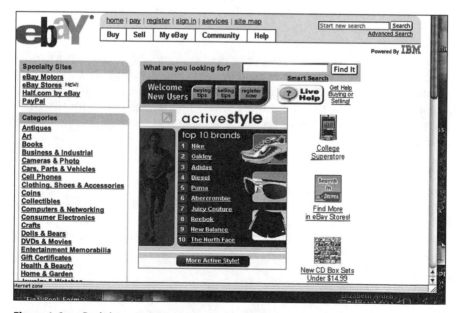

Figure 1-2   eBay's home page prompts you to search, buy, or sell an item and register as a first-time user or sign in as an eBay member.

What Does It Mean to Be Sniped at an Auction?

When you've been *sniped* at an auction, this means that you've been outbid in the last few seconds. This usually only happens on online auctions such as eBay. A service now exists called Auction Sniper that automatically places your eBay bid for you in the last seconds of the auction, thus increasing your chances of winning. A small fee is charged for this service when you win. To learn more, go to www.AuctionSniper.com.

What Is an Auction with Reserve?

An *auction with reserve* means that the item will not sell unless it reaches a predetermined value set by the seller. When an item meets the reserve price, that item will sell for that reserve price or higher. Usually, entire auctions are held with reserve unless the terms state that the auction is unreserved (where the item or property sells to the highest bidder, no matter what the conditions, such as weather, crowd attendance, etc.).

What Does As Is, Where Is Mean?

The phrase "as is, where is" is used at real estate foreclosure sales and personal property auctions. The auction is based on the buyer's inspection of the property or the item up for sale. In other words, when a buyer purchases something, he is discouraged from returning the item even if the buyer finds something wrong with the property or the item after it is sold. Some auction houses are flexible on their return policy, and others are not.

What Is a Buyer's Premium?

A *buyer's premium* is a percentage that is added onto the final sale price of an item. For instance, when you purchase something for $100 and the buyer's premium is 10 percent, you must pay an additional $10, or $110 (plus applicable sales tax if you're not a dealer). Buyer's premiums range from 10 to 20 percent. Usually, the auctioneer keeps the buyer's premium as part of the expenses incurred.

What Is a Sale by Catalog or Numbered Order?

Some auction houses will categorize the merchandise for sale by lot numbers and sell consecutively in order with a catalog number for each item. At some auction houses, you have to pay for these catalogs, which range from very informal sheets of paper stapled together for $5 or less to catalogs with color pictures for $20 to $50.

What Does Numbers at 7:00 A.M. Mean?

A preferred method of doing business by some professional estate companies and others is to give out numbers an hour ahead of the sale. You take a number, much like you do at the deli counter of the grocery store. If you're first in

GOOD LUCK

Speaking of elephants, take note of the trunk. Trunks pointing up signify good luck, and trunks pointing down signify bad luck. I have purchased both types and can tell you that whether they're ceramic, plaster, or carved wood, elephants with their trunks in the sky sell better (see Figure 1-3).

line, you will get the first number. You can leave, but you must return promptly at the designated sale time or you will lose your place. The professionals will only let in so many numbers at a time (sometimes 1 to 25 or fewer). The most common reasons are to ensure crowd control in small apartments or houses and to discourage theft.

What Is a White Elephant Table?

Church bazaars or church fairs often advertise a white elephant table. *White elephant* is a term for an item that is useless to someone but valuable to someone else. White elephants do exist, but they are rare and expensive to keep.

Figure 1-3   An elephant with its trunk up, like the one shown here, is more valuable.

The white elephant tables usually are loaded with knickknacks, china, glass, jewelry, and generally items that are smaller than a breadbox. Go to these sales because once in a while you'll find a rare white elephant.

The Early Bird Special

The familiar saying, "The early bird catches the worm," most certainly applies to anyone who wants to find that next "Antiques Roadshow" treasure.

TIP: Adhere to the old saying, "Early to bed, early to rise, makes a man healthy, wealthy, and wise."

What Is an Early Bird?

An *early bird* is anyone who shows up early at a sale (dealers or nondealers) before the advertised time. This generally means that buyers will arrive anywhere from one to three hours before the start of a sale.

What If the Ad Says, "Early Birds Welcome"?

Take advantage of this invitation and go to the sale early. Arrive at 5:30 A.M. even if you have to wait until 6:00 A.M. for the seller to appear. Of course, you're not obligated to buy or stay. You can peruse the sale and then go onto the next one if this one doesn't have anything worth purchasing.

What If the Ad Says, "Early Birds Pay Double"?

Sellers who don't want early birds knocking at their door will explicitly say in their ad, "Early Birds Pay Double." They don't want to deal with people showing up three hours before the start of their sale. If you arrive early and a bureau is marked $100, you will have to pay $200 for it. *Note:* Not all sellers will stick to their advertisement, and you may walk away with a prize.

What If the Ad Says, "No Early Birds" (Sometimes Abbreviated as NEB)?

Some sellers will advertise "No Early Birds" in the newspaper and/or post a sign near the entrance to their property (see Figure 1-4). Go to these sales despite the signage because (1) most other people avoid going early to these sales and (2) you may get into the sale just for that reason.

The Price Is Right

Everyone wants a bargain. But if you think the item is already at a bargain price, should you ask the seller, "What's your best price?" If you're an early bird, do you still ask for a lower price?" Part II: The Basics of Buying will answer these questions in more depth.

Figure 1-4   A "No Early Birds" sign keeps dealers and others away until the sale officially starts.

TIP: My mother, Barbara Glass, a garage sale aficionado and auctioneer says that when buying an item "Be aware that 'beauty is in the eye of the beholder' and often reflected in the price."

What If Nothing Is Priced at a Garage Sale?
Then ask for a price on something that you want to buy. Don't wait until the seller tags the items. Some sellers never tag anything and instead suggest you make an offer. Grab hold of something that catches your eye. Did you spot more than one item? Place those items in your tote bag or start a "sold" section and cover your intended purchases with your jacket. Chapter 6 gives you tips on how to scoop up the bargains quickly.

What If the Seller Says, "Make Me an Offer"?
You go to a sale and know that you can make a profit on something you see. You ask, "How much is this?" The seller replies, "Make me an offer." What do you do, (a) give the seller a dollar, (b) offer a fair price, or (c) say, "I don't know what it's worth. What were you thinking?" See Chapter 7 to learn why all three answers are correct.

What If the Seller Says, "I Have More Magazines in the Attic"?
What do you say? Smile and say, "I'd be happy to take a look," even though you don't want any magazines. Why? Chapter 9 gives the reason as well as other ways to get inside the house to find more treasures.

I Don't Know if the Prices on These Antiques Are High or Low.
What Should I Do?
Go to as many auctions, estate sales, flea markets, and antique shows as your schedule allows. Go to eBay and surf the categories and recently sold prices for various types of antiques. Read price guides and reference books. Chapter 10 helps you to decide whether or not you should specialize in an area that interests you.

Show Me the Money

Cash talks, especially in this business. When you make an offer, be bold, but polite. Often rudeness will rub the seller the wrong way, and he may not sell you anything, no matter what amount of money you offer. Graciously, have the correct amount of money visible so the seller is tempted to make the deal.

Can I Pay by Check or Credit Card?
Regarding garage sales, yard sales, and the like, sellers prefer cash. If you're going to a local sale at a church or club in your community, a local check is usually okay. Some estate sales run by professionals are equipped to take credit cards. However, most of the time sellers prefer cash. At auctions, you may have to pay cash until you establish credit to write a check. Some auction companies will take credit cards but boost the buyer's premium up 2 to 3 percent more to cover the credit card fees.

Can I Leave a Deposit?
Once in awhile, you can leave a deposit. Let someone in charge know your intentions, and ask for a receipt, even for a partial payment. Then find a bank or automatic teller machine (ATM) to get the full amount of cash, return to the sale, and pay for your item in full.

Is Trucking Available?
Usually at a garage sale you have to remove furniture yourself, although some sellers will help you load, or even deliver a heavy piece of furniture or a bedroom set. Negotiate a fair delivery charge or tip them if they refuse to take any money. Most auction companies also have a trucking service available for a fee. Ask a member of the auction staff before the auction starts so that you know how long you have for removal and if you have to arrange for trucking yourself.

Sell, Sell, Sell

Now that you've bought, bought, bought, you must sell, sell, and sell. Follow the philosophy of the New York Stock Exchange—"Buy low, sell high!" Part III of this book discusses making your big profit and the many selling venues open to you.

TIP: "A fool and his money are soon parted." Take risks, but don't buy and sell foolishly.

Trash or Treasure?

This is the important question, and this is why research is mandatory. You want to make sure that if you find a treasure, you don't sell it for trash. Chapter 12 discusses a number of authorities you can work with to evaluate your finds. Chapter 15 has true stories from dealers, "junkies," and others who have hit it big and their insider tips for the beginner. Figure 1-5 gives an example of a lamp that was once thought of as undesirable and thrown out in the trash in the 1930s and 40s.

Figure 1-5 Tiffany lamps, once regarded as trash, are now considered valuable treasures. Rare patterns bring upwards of $100,000 at aucti 35on. This one is a handmade recreation, but the shade depicts the famous Tiffany dragonfly pattern. *(Photo courtesy of designer Dee Dee Corey of www.Northeasternlamps.com.)*

BREAKFAST AT TIFFANY'S

Tiffany is a definite must-buy. Louis Comfort Tiffany was a famous New York City designer of exquisite stained glass lamps, iridescent glass vases, jewelry, and silver. His designs were produced from the late 1800s to the early 1930s. Many of Tiffany's pieces are signed LCT, Tiffany & Co., Tiffany Favrile, and Tiffany Studios as well as numbered.

How Do I Research an Item?

Chapter 11 helps you to understand the market of antiques and collectibles. Trends exist. Fads come and go. Some antiques that are hot today are useless tomorrow. Other antiques are reproduced and sold as reproductions, and that usually reduces the value of the original antique. You will learn how to evaluate pricing based on price guides, eBay, and auctions. Learn the difference between show prices and consignment prices when you sell your goods.

Where Do I Sell My Treasures?

Today, many options exist. eBay is one of the most lucrative and accessible places to sell your valuables all over the world. Auctions and antique shows are other viable marketplaces. Chapters 12 and 13 review the varied places to sell your purchases, places you may not have considered until now. Chapter 12 discusses selling through the experts, such as auctions, co-ops, and consignment galleries. Chapter 13 discusses selling on your own, including classified ads, eBay, flea markets, and your own garage or yard sales.

When You Cross the Bridge

You cross over the bridge from hobbyist to lobbyist when

- Saturday garage sale shopping becomes a weekend obsession—every weekend.
- Auction fever has you sweating, or waiting on pins and needles for the next big estate auction in your area.
- Your garage or basement is chock full of merchandise, and you know that you can't fit in another piece—well, maybe just one more piece.

However, going from part time to full time is a big step. You have to think about organization, inventory, mailing, advertising, ethics, taxes, and more.

TIP: If someone tries to sell you a bridge, it's probably a skilled dealer or a fast-talking auctioneer. If you're trying to sell a bridge, congratulations, you've graduated from part-time to full-time valedictorian.

Is What I'm Doing Ethical?

An unspoken code of ethics exists, especially among dealers, when you go to garage or estate sales, and I'll discuss this code in my book. Ethical questions also arise when you buy and sell certain types of items, such as guns, knives, furs, and Nazi memorabilia. Chapter 14 gives several examples and one case that went to court to decide ownership of an item purchased at a yard sale.

What About Taxes?

Unfortunately, you can't avoid taxes and the paperwork involved when you resell what you buy. Don't wait until the night before taxes are due to figure out your net profit and inventory carryover. Chapter 14 talks about taxes and gives tips on finding a good accountant if you're not proficient with numbers.

When Should I Go Full Time?

Buying and selling may turn into something more than a fascinating part-time hobby when

- You make more money at garage sales on the weekend than you make all week at your current job.
- You eat, sleep, breathe, and dream about garage sale and auction treasures.
- You have a burning desire to work for yourself instead of at someone else's shop or auction.

You can do it. I'll show you how in Chapter 14.

I hope some of these answers have satisfied or piqued your curiosity by now to read more. We'll spend the rest of this book exploring all these topics in depth so that you may have great success buying—and reselling—other people's junk. Are you ready? Let's suit up.

2

Gearing Up

Whether you're getting ready for a Saturday morning garage sale, a flea market, or an auction, you need to wear and bring certain tools to maximize your buying experience and thus your profits. Leave the designer jeans and $200 name-brand running shoes at home. Put on an old pair of jeans and a baggy sweatshirt. Ladies, forget about your hair and makeup. And guys, don't shave! In this chapter I'll discuss what to wear, what to bring, and other techniques for successful preparation.

YOUR BUYING ATTIRE

When you participate in certain sports and activities, the proper outfit for that activity is an essential requirement of the game. For example, if you're going scuba diving, you have a specific array of gear to put on—wetsuit, flippers, tank, mask, etc. If you're a serious garage sale hunter or auction sleuth, certain gear is needed to put you at the top of your game (see Figure 2-1). Your attire should consist of the following:

- Sweats or old jeans
- Jacket or sweater
- Sneakers or walking shoes
- Sunglasses
- Hat

Sweats or Old Jeans

You will get dirty going through other people's stuff, so wear an old pair of sweats or jeans. Wear something comfortable with pockets. An extra stash of

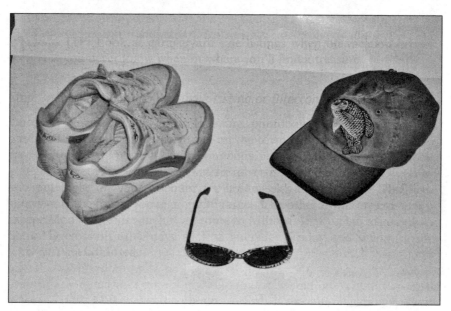

Figure 2-1 Attire for the serious buyer.

cash in your front pocket is added security when you find that Heywood-Wakefield 10-piece wicker porch set at a church sale.

Jacket or Sweater

Wearing a sweat jacket or sweater allows you to dress in layers. At 6 A.M., the air may be chilly, but by ten o'clock on a warm day, you can break out in a sweat. If you go to an on-site auction, and the sale is advertised rain or shine, bring a rain jacket just in case you are subject to the elements.

Sneakers or Walking Shoes

A garage sale is often a race from start to finish. Wear a good pair of sneakers. You won't believe the amount of walking you will do in a day. At some auctions, you stand on cement or walk all day, so comfortable shoes are a must.

Sunglasses

I know it sounds like we should go to the beach, but the intentions are much different. You should wear sunglasses to conceal your identity so that you can buy at a sale before your competition turns around and realizes that they have

THE 50-YARD DASH

Every Labor Day weekend, the historical society in my town has a sale in the carriage sheds on the town common. The sale starts at 10 A.M. on Saturday. Officials rope off half the parking lot so that no one can enter. A few minutes before opening, the officials take the rope down, but no one is allowed to take a step until the church bell rings. The idea is to give everyone a fair chance, but it's such a mad dash to reach the merchandise that you need to wear good running shoes. Keep this in mind if your town has a similar sale.

to buy faster because you're going to get all the best items first. See Chapter 8 on other ways to stay ahead of the competition. And more important, the glare from the sun on glassware or aluminum dishes may cause you to miss something valuable at a sale if the light blinds you.

Hat

A hat is a smart accessory if you stand out in the sun for a long time. It's not uncommon to stand in line for an hour or two before you're allowed into an estate or church sale. A hat is also a handy carrying device for small knick-knacks if you forget your bag. At some outside auctions, tents are not set up, so you must either find a shade tree or bake in the sun.

TEN ACCESSORIES FOR BETTER BUYING

The most important items to bring with you are accessories that you actually want to attach to your body (see Figure 2-2) so that your hands are free to pick up merchandise that you intend to buy.

1. Money in small bills
2. Tummy pack or money belt
3. Empty tote bag
4. Magnifying glass or loop
5. Tape measure
6. Flashlight
7. Magnet
8. Pen and notepad
9. Pocket calculator
10. Labels

Figure 2-2   Accessories for the serious shopper.

1. Money

Obviously, you need money to buy. As a beginner, you can start with as little as $20. If you can afford $100, that's even better. For garage sales or flea markets, I carry $500 in my tummy pack, with at least $50 in one-dollar bills and then a mixture of five-, ten-, and twenty-dollar bills. In addition, I have one or two $100 bills tucked in a separate pocket. I also keep an extra $500 locked in the glove box in my van.

   If you find a really good buy, you never want to run short on money. Seasoned pros will carry several thousand dollars in their pocket. As a backup, have your checkbook and credit card available. Some auction houses will let you write a local check or use a credit card. Always ask ahead of time for payment terms at an auction.

   TIP: When scurrying from garage sale to garage sale, carry plenty of one-dollar bills and a pocketful of change. If possible, give each seller the exact amount of money for your purchase so that you can hurry to the next sale.

   Believe it or not, at some tag sales or church sales, you can still buy items for 5, 10, and 25 cents. If your pouch is full of change, you can pay the cashier quickly. When the line is long, especially at church sales, and the cashier has added up the price to be $14.65, hand her $15.00 and say, "Keep the change for the church." She's grateful, and you're grateful to go to the next sale.

2. Tummy Pack or Money Belt

The easiest way to carry money is to wear a money belt or tummy pack that buckles around your waist. (A purse slips off your shoulder, and a wallet requires two hands to access money.) The reasons to wear a tummy pack are

- Both hands are free to pick up and examine items.
- Your money is within easy reach.
- Ladies, you don't have to worry about keeping track of your purse when you're at an auction.

3. Empty Tote Bag

In case you see numerous items you want to buy, a tote bag is a very handy item to have and will serve the purpose better than a box. A box will limit your ability to gather more items. A tote bag, even if you've filled it with several items, can be placed on your arm so that both hands are free to pick up more items. You also can use a tote bag at a "cash and carry" auction where you must take possession of items you just bid on. For example, you may buy small items at an in-house walk-around auction or an auction held in a field where you can't leave your purchases unattended. A tote bag or two will put your mind at ease if you must grab hold of an item once it is sold to you.

4. Magnifying Glass or Loop

A magnifying glass or loop will help you discern between "14K" (real gold) and "14K GF" (abbreviation for gold-filled, which is not as valuable). A loop is a small device that fits in your eye socket and has a magnification power of 10× or 20×. For the same reason, if your doctor has prescribed bifocals or glasses, wear them. Don't let vanity stand in the way of a good deal. Wear the loop around your neck, or put the magnifying glass in your back pocket. Some magnifying glasses are also equipped with a light for those dark corners in the house or garage. Often, auction companies will let you borrow the house magnifying glass or loop.

TIP: Experienced dealers also carry diamond testers, gold testers, and grams and pennyweight scales to thoroughly evaluate an item they want to purchase. If you become involved in buying jewelry, you may want to consider investing in these tools.

MEASURING UP

A Windsor chair is a specific style of a New England chair originally made in the late 1700s to the early 1800s (see Figure 2-3). E. B. Tracy of (Lisbon) Norwich, Connecticut, signed many of the Windsor chairs he made. These old, original chairs will command upwards of $1,000 from the serious collector. Sometimes a dealer will use a tape measure to see if the height of a Windsor chair has been cut down, although most seasoned pros can tell at a glance if the chair is the correct height.

5. Tape Measure

A tape measure is useful to see if that awkward table is going to fit in your car or if you have to position it through the sunroof or rent a truck. Hitch the tape measure to your waist for quick accessibility.

TIP: Early tables or stands that were made square may no longer measure square because of wood shrinkage. A 24 by 24-inch square top table may shrink to 23½ by 24 inches. An uneven size is a strong indication that you have an old piece as opposed to a reproduction.

Figure 2-3 An example of a reproduction Windsor chair. An original one from the 1700s is worth thousands of dollars.

6. Flashlight

Sometimes garages are dark, even with the lights on in broad daylight. A flashlight will come in handy if you are out before dawn. Clip it onto your pocket, or wear it around your neck. At an on-site auction, if the light is poor, use the flashlight to read names etched into pieces of china and glass or labels on the backs of chairs or bureaus. Most auction houses have adequate lighting facilities. Some buyers, for example, art dealers, carry a black light (see Figure 2-4) to detect any repairs, new paint, and authentic signatures on paintings.

TIP: A flashlight is a handy accessory when you go to flea markets before dawn. Flashlight shoppers scurry to each vendor in search of that hidden treasure or bargain. If you observed this event from above, the flea market would resemble a field full of fireflies.

7. Magnet

Carry a magnet in your pocket to check to see if an item is brass or bronze. A magnet won't stick to either of these materials. A magnet will stick to iron or

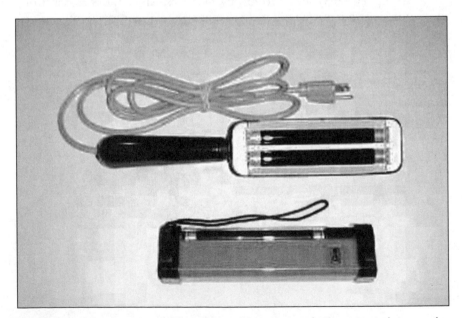

Figure 2-4 Some buyers carry black lights, either power or battery operated, to examine artwork.

steel. Sometimes, if an item is painted, you can't tell the underlying substance. Brass or bronze items are more desirable, and you could find a valuable vase or urn worth hundreds or thousands of dollars.

8. Pen and Notepad

If you're buying at 20 different sales on a Saturday, have a pen and notepad to keep track of your purchases. Record how much you paid for an item and the date and address of the sale. You also can use the notepad to jot down a signature or mark to look up in your reference books at a later date. Once in a while you need the notepad for a lead to go look at a houseful of merchandise. At an auction, you can use the back of your bid number to record purchases or use the notebook if the auction is a pay by cash as you go sale.

9. Pocket Calculator

In case you buy a boxful of items at a yard sale, and the cashier isn't equipped to add up the items, pull out your pocket calculator and offer to do the addition on the calculator together.

Keep track of your purchases at an auction, and calculate the total before paying the cashier.

10. Labels

Keep 5 to 10 address-size labels in your money belt. Have some blank labels and some preprinted labels with your name and the word "SOLD" in bold letters. For example, mark your labels, "Sold to G.G." At an estate or furniture sale, you can quickly place your label on items you intend to purchase. This is faster than trying to find the seller, who may be standing near the exit door. You can also use these labels to mark your purchases at an auction. Some auction companies have their own sold tags, and some companies do not. Note: Sold labels won't keep someone from walking off with your table, but it is a deterrent.

THIRTEEN ITEMS TO KEEP IN YOUR CAR

Whether you go to an auction, a flea market, or a yard sale, keep these items in your car when you go on a weekend buying jaunt:

1. Newspapers
2. Empty boxes
3. Blankets
4. Rope or bungie cords
5. Your treasure map (for garage sales)

6. Street or road map
7. Umbrella
8. Sunscreen/bug spray
9. Wipes
10. Reference books/price guides
11. Cell phone/laptop computer
12. Fuel for your car
13. Fuel for yourself

Here's why.

1. Newspapers

The two types of newspapers you need are

- One or two current local editions
- A stack of older editions

The most important newspaper is the one with the most current local and/or weekly classified section. Most classified sections of newspapers have a listing for "Garage or Yard Sales" and a listing of "Auctions." Some papers distinguish the garage or yard sale listings with a pair of scissors and dotted lines around the entire section. Take this hint, and cut out the listings so that you don't have to carry the entire paper with you.

Keep a stack of older newspapers in your car to wrap up any fragile items you purchase. Bubble wrap or packing peanuts will work, too. But newspapers are cheap, readily available, and take up little space.

2. Empty Boxes

You'll need three or four boxes in which to store your purchases. Place the newspapers in one of the empty boxes, and put the other empty boxes in your car. Often, sellers don't have boxes to give you, and you don't want to scramble around looking for one when you're at a garage sale. Some auction companies keep a supply of empty boxes and newspapers for their buying customers.

TIP: To save valuable time at a garage sale, never let a seller wrap your purchases. When a seller offers to wrap your items, politely say, "I have newspaper and boxes in the car." If you wait to have your purchases wrapped, you'll waste valuable time. You want to get in and out of a sale as quickly as possible. Sellers don't think you're in a rush. Why would you be? You're at their sale! They're having a good time, and they think you're having a good time, too.

3. Blankets

Always carry three or four blankets or furniture pads in your car. You can wrap and pad furniture so that it won't get scratched. Wrap any delicate items you purchase, such as mirrors or lamps, in these blankets.

4. Rope or Bungee Cords

To secure furniture that you've purchased, have several lengths of rope or several bungee cords in your car. Tie the pieces in your van or on top of your car. If you drive too fast, stop short for any reason, or hit any bumps, you could have more dents, dings, and scratches in the item by the time you get home than when you bought it.

5. Your Treasure Map (for Garage Sales)

The most important map when you're on the hunt for garage sale treasures is the one that you plotted the day or night before the sale. This treasure map is marked up with all the advertised sales you've seen in the listings in the newspaper. I'll show you how to chart an effective treasure map in Chapter 4. Keep this map in eye's view on the passenger seat.

6. Street or Road Map

Always have a local street and state map in your car in case you run across an unadvertised sale or need to double-check the auction address. Finding and attending sales in cities and urban areas is a challenge because of one-way streets, construction work, and limited parking. If you anticipate these kinds of delays, give yourself extra time. You could have a friend read the map to you as you drive to the destination, but often you're alone.

Your other choices are MapQuest or Navigator. MapQuest provides free maps and driving directions. Go to www.mapquest.com/directions, and enter both the starting and destination addresses. You will have access to a map with the most direct route along with written directions. Navigator is a navigational system that uses satellite technology and a digital map to help you determine your exact position (in case you get lost going to a sale). Some cars are equipped with this feature, or you can purchase a portable navigator that plugs into your cigarette lighter for under $1,000.

7. Umbrella

The umbrella is handy when you have to wait outside in the pouring rain until a garage sale starts. Before the doors open, however, collapse the umbrella and shove it in your trench coat. Better yet, wear a raincoat with a hood. You don't want to fumble around with an umbrella, a flashlight, and money while

STREET AND LANE ARE NOT THE SAME!

Once I drove in circles trying to find a garage sale because I thought it was at 22 Buttercup Lane when it was really at 22 Buttercup Street. When I arrived at 22 Buttercup Lane, the lights were out, and the garage had disappeared. I double-checked the ad, and it said Buttercup Street. Thus, by the time I found the sale, the items were not so sweet. *Note:* Sometimes the error is in the newspaper advertisement.

trying to hold onto a glass vase that almost fell out of your arm because you were soaked.

TIP: A garbage bag will serve a double-duty purpose: (1) as a spare bag in which to carry your merchandise and (2) as a makeshift raincoat in the event of a sudden downpour.

8. Sunscreen/Bug Spray

When the black flies or mosquitoes swarm in the early morning, bug spray will ward off those pesky creatures. Sunscreen will prevent burns on a hot, sunny day. A combination of bug spray and sunscreen will keep you happy all day. Apply these remedies before you go on your buying spree. You won't remember to lotion up when you're on a frantic treasure hunt at a townwide yard sale event.

9. Wipes

A supply of wet wipes or baby wipes is a standard commodity in your car if you have kids. No kids? Buy a box of wipes anyway. They're great to take the grime off your hands in between sales or after you're done with your auction for the day. Use a wet wipe to clean a piece of pottery to read the mark on the bottom or to wipe the glass on a picture frame to read the artist's signature.

10. Reference Books/Price Guides

If you're serious about buying and selling for profit, keep three or four reference books in your car. A resource book and/or price guide is available for nearly every interest. Price guides are discussed in depth in Chapter 11.

11. Cell Phone/Laptop Computer

Since we live in the age of technology, a cell phone and, ideally, a laptop computer are definite advantages when you buy and sell for several reasons.

1. You can call for assistance if your automobile breaks down.
2. You can call for help if you sense an uncomfortable buying situation when you're alone with a stranger in his house.
3. You can phone a friend or expert in the field for his opinion on an item about which you're unsure of as to its value or authenticity.
4. You can shoot a photo, if you have a camera phone, of an item up for auction and send it instantly to a colleague to research or to an expert for his opinion.
5. You can hook up to the Internet with your wireless phone and laptop computer to research the market value of a particular collectible or antique, or to find out further information regarding an artist or a designer.

12. Fuel for Your Car

Nothing is more frustrating than getting in your car to discover that your gas tank is on empty. What's worse is that you have to stop at a gas station at 6 A.M., pump in $20, and watch Dealer Jack shoot past you with his pedal to the metal, trying to beat you to the next sale. So check your engine, your oil, your tires, and your gas tank (preferably the day before).

Carry your auto club membership card in case you break down in unfamiliar territory. For business purposes, you will need an auto mileage log to record your mileage. You could travel 200 to 500 miles on a Saturday morning to track down yard sales or attend an out-of-state country auction. These miles add up over the course of a year, and you should consider deducting the mileage and the use of your vehicle when you file your taxes.

TIP: As you buy more merchandise, you may want to upgrade to a van or truck or borrow a friend's truck for the weekend. For diehard auction or estate sale goers, why not sleep in your van and be comfortable!

13. Fuel for Yourself

Don't forget to tank yourself up. Pack a snack, such as a cereal bar or fruit, something to keep you focused and energized when you go for the gold. Are you a coffee drinker? Program the coffee pot the night before so that you're on autopilot at the crack of dawn. Are the Boy Scouts selling coffee and doughnuts at a sale? Don't succumb unless the line is short and you can buy a treat in a flash. If you don't drink caffeine or eat sweets, have some juice, an energy drink, a piece of fruit, or a bottle of water to give yourself that extra jolt to start your engine and keep you going!

GEARED UP

Now you know what to wear:

- Old jeans, sunglasses, and a hat

And what to bring:

- Tote bag, flashlight, and magnifying glass

And what to keep handy in your car:

- Empty boxes, newspapers, cell phone, and several price guides

So let the race begin. On your mark, get set, go. And you're off.

3

Learning the Trade Names

Types of sales are as varied as the cities or countryside in which you find them. The most common sales are *garage* and *yard sales.* Some sale names may signal regional locations, such as the *tag sale* in the suburbs. Maine holds *porch sales* on Thursday. Minnesota has *yard sales* Wednesday through Sunday. A sale that started long ago in New England was the *penny sale,* where every item for sale cost a penny. Other places where you can find bargains are also mentioned, including auctions, eBay, flea markets, pawnshops, and thrift stores. No matter what you call them or where they are, they all have a potential treasure waiting for you to discover. This chapter will explore various types of sales, including which ones are great for beginners and for seasoned buyers.

TOP SIX SALES TO TARGET

If you're new to the idea of buying something for resale, target these top six sales. They will give you the most variety and best places to search for treasures.

- Townwide
- Estate
- Moving
- Church
- Multifamily
- Neighborhood

As you gain experience, your preferences may change. Some dealers will only go to estate sales. For them, all other sales are a waste of time. Other dealers will go to the townwide or citywide sales no matter what else is going on that day.

TOP THREE AUCTIONS TO TARGET

If you're starting out at auctions, target these types of auctions first:

- Estate
- On-site
- Consignment

If you're targeting online auctions, search out these sites first:

- eBay
- Yahoo! Auctions
- Your Favorite Auction Company

A TO Z SALES

Now let's discuss the various types of sales. For easy reference, this list of A to Z sales is in alphabetical order so that when you put together your treasure map, you can quickly reference the sales you see in the paper.

Annual Sale

Sellers often advertise these sales using the word *annual* to let buyers know that they've had these sales before, such as "Annual Memorial Day Weekend Sale." Sometimes a seller will advertise a "First Annual Sale." Often these once-a-year sales become second-, third-, fourth-, or fifth-year sales and will be advertised as "Fifth Annual Yard Sale." And each year they get bigger and bigger. Libraries often will advertise "Annual Library Book Sale." If you've never attended an annual sale, go to one. Some dealers make note of the annual sales where they've made successful purchases and attend every year.

Antique Show and Sale

Traditionally, any item over 100 years old is an antique. Dealers who close or reduce inventory in their shops often hold antique sales. Antique shows are held throughout the country all year long. The most famous antique show on the East Coast, known as "Brimfield," is held outdoors three times a year (May, July, and September) in Brimfield, Massachusetts. The event hosts 5,000 dealers and lasts six days, with 20 different shows opening on certain days all week long. People travel from all over the country and Europe to buy and sell at this landmark event (see Figure 3-1). For the beginner, this is a great place to learn about antiques. For the seasoned pro, you can test your knowledge and discover unusual or unique antiques from around the world.

Figure 3-1 Brimfield, Massachusetts, hosts the most famous antique show on the East Coast.

Attic Sale

When someone advertises an attic sale, plan to arrive at the sale early because *attic* indicates an accumulation of old, stored, and antique items. Expect to find untold surprises and a treasure or two. A sale advertised as an attic sale rarely will ever get you into the attic. Rather, items are brought out of the attic and displayed on the lawn or in the garage. Churches often have a table or two set up as "Attic Treasures" when they have their bazaars or harvest fairs. These sales are worth attending, especially if the church members are older, because older members tend to have items of value that they've had in the family for years. To get into the attic, read Chapter 9.

Auctions

Controversy still exists today over whether an auction is a sale or not, but the main distinction is that, for the most part, buyers actually determine the fair market value of an item by bidding against each other. We could say, "All's fair in love and war."

Auctions run the gamut from small on-site household sales in the country (see Figure 3-2) to prestigious art and antique auctions in major cities. And don't forget about farm, auto, tobacco, horse, and real estate auctions. Many

Figure 3-2 An on-site auction draws a large crowd with a variety of merchandise for the avid collector and bargain hunter.

great buys are made at auctions and resold to private collectors or museums. And vice versa. Many great items are sold at auction and set new world records.

If you're a beginner, don't shy away from auctions. Before the sale, tell the auctioneer that this is your first auction and ask, "How does this work?" Most auctioneers are glad to answer your questions because they are looking for new customers also.

If you're a seasoned pro, you may want to try your hand at buying at storage auctions. Often the entire contents of a storage unit are sold, sight unseen, and you have to be willing to gamble that you may find one great item packed away among clothes and pots and pans. Check the newspaper for these types of sales.

Barn Sale

A barn sale conjures up the meaning of the words *old and forgotten.* Farm equipment, saddles, tin signs, eighteenth-century furniture, folk art items, books, baskets, and tools are a few of the items you'll find at a barn sale. Plan to arrive early at these sales because they get crowded quickly. These sales are a gold mine for seasoned dealers, who target them early because they know that they may unearth a seventeenth-century pilgrim chair or an early tavern table tucked in the corner covered with hay.

Book Sale

Churches and libraries have book sales regularly and advertise them as a "Library Book Sale" or a "Book Sale at St. John's Church." If you love books, this is an area where you may want to concentrate. Beware that many book dealers and collectors will target these sales first. You will find a huge variety from hard covers to paperbacks to sets. Most book sales are well organized, and the books are sorted by categories with signs at each table. Categories include antiques, children's books, classics, cookbooks, gardening books, history, military books, magic, music, nature, textbooks, wine, etc. If you have a particular interest or knowledge in a subject, seek out that table.

Hardcover books can range from $1.00 to $25 each and up. Paperbacks are usually 10 cents to $1.00 each. At the end of the day, buyers often can fill a paper bag for $1.00. Even if you arrive late at a sale, don't rule out the possibility of finding a bargain. One woman I know buys children's books and resells them on eBay. She buys most of them for under $1.00 when everyone else has finished picking over the books and sells them on eBay for $5.00 or more. This may not seem like much, but she ships out 50 to 100 books a week.

TIP: Request to be on the church or library mailing list for these specific events. Check your local phone book, and call the librarian and/or the church secretary and ask to be placed on the mailing list for upcoming events.

Church Bazaar or Fair

Church sales, especially seasonal bazaars or fairs, frequently occur in the spring or from October to December. Some churches will post notices on the drive by bulletin boards on their front lawn weeks in advance. You'll find a vast array of merchandise at church bazaars, often with other vendors selling new items and crafts. Skip the baked goods and the homemade teddy bear tables. Zoom in on the tables with items that you can resell at a profit. These sales are great for both the beginner and the seasoned pro. If you're just starting out, observe what other professionals quickly scoop up.

TIP: At a church sale, go directly to the "jewelry," "white elephant," or "attic treasures" tables. Why? These tables are more likely to have antiques, china, glass, silver, and jewelry that you can buy for a few dollars and sell for much more.

Club Sale

Watch for these key words—*to benefit Kiwanis, Girl Scouts, Boy Scouts, Elks, Fire Department, Humane Society, Lions Club,* etc. Usually this type of sale signifies a mixture of old and new merchandise because the membership base is so large. You have a 90 percent chance of finding at least one item that you can resell. Many people will contribute to these clubs and organizations to support the cause. Because the quantity of merchandise is usually so extensive, beginners and pros are apt to find new and old merchandise to buy and resell.

TIP: Many churches and clubs will offer a free pickup service to members or donors. The donors will tend to give the church more donations if they don't have to move the merchandise themselves. A jackpot of treasures could emerge from someone's basement or attic.

Craft Sale

When you think of a craft sale, you think of new and handmade items for sale. Craft sales are ubiquitous during the holidays. Items of value that you can find and sell for profit at craft sales include old postcards, valentines, old lace, old material, buttons, and containers such as old baskets, pottery, tin, and bottles. Sometimes old quilts are mixed in with new quilts. Look for hand-sewn and appliqué quilts such as the log cabin, Dresden plate, and Sunbonnet Babies, to name a few. Even old patchwork pieces have value. Again, condition is everything. Make sure that the quilt is not soiled or torn extensively.

TIP: Many crafters will use old items to display new and useful items in, often not realizing the value of the older pieces. Be sure to look at the containers holding items, and don't hesitate to ask if they are for sale as well.

eBay

eBay is the leader in online auction companies. To quote numbers (over tens of millions as of this writing) would not do any good because the number of registered users changes daily. eBay is worldwide; for example, it has become the dominant online auction company in Asia. Just about anything can be bought and sold on eBay. It has its forbidden categories (such

A BASKET CASE!

One Saturday, my mother, Barbara, and I were driving along Route 4 in Maine when we saw a sign that said, "Turn right, Craft Sale two miles." We wondered why someone would have a craft sale down an old country road. We suspected that most of the items would be ceramic pots, dried flowers, baskets, patterns, and bric-a-brac. But we decided to go anyway, and we weren't alone. Other people were already milling around. I went to the plant table, and my mother went to the basket table. She found a small, tightly woven Indian basket in very good condition. The vendor didn't realize its value, hence the 50-cent price tag. However, the basket turned out to be an authentic period piece. My mom sold the basket a few months later at an antique auction for $225.

as firearms and alcohol), but the eBay market is everchanging. For fun, click on the eBay Web site at www.eBay.com, and type in any kind of item you can think of, and it is probably being sold this week. And probably more than one item in the same category is being offered as well (see Figure 3-3). To really understand the world of eBay, read Dennis L. Prince's

145 items found for **Lunch Boxes**		· Add to Favorites		
List View | Picture Gallery	Sort by: Price: highest first ⬍	Customize Display		
	Item Title	**Price ▾**	**Bids**	**Time Left**
☐	🖼 julia lunch boxes 🔎	$600.00	-	6d 17h 48m
☐	FOUR OLD LUNCH BOXES ,LONE RANGER,BIONIC WOMAN 🔎📷	$99.00	-	4d 15h 40m
☐	Old SUPER POWERS/SPEED BUGGY/ THUNDERCATS LUNCH BOXES 🔎📷	$46.66	7	2d 01h 12m
☐	1978 Star Wars and 1983 ROTJ Metal Lunch Boxes	$41.50	21	1h 10m
☐	Set of 2 Collectible Mickey Mouse Lunch Boxes 🔎📷	$31.00	12	23h 15m
☐	Superman Lunch Box Lot! 3 Different Lunch Boxes! 🔎	$19.99	-	2d 01h 49m
☐	3 Superman & Spiderman & Batman Lunch Boxes! DEAL! 🔎	$19.99	-	3d 16h 14m

Figure 3-3 eBay has hundreds of categories. Type in one particular item and see how many similar items are offered on any given day or week.

book, *How to Sell Anything on eBay and Make a Fortune,* published by McGraw-Hill.

TIP: eBay is a good place to go "junking" if you are elderly, disabled, or confined indoors owing to inclement weather or have no transportation. eBay is the ultimate garage sale all year round.

Estate Sale

Estate sales are a gold mine for buyers. Almost all estate sales are just that—an entire estate, meaning in many cases that you are allowed to tour an entire house or most of it. In some instances, if the estate is small or the owners don't want people in the house, the sale will be billed as an "Estate/Yard Sale," and furniture and other items will be displayed on the lawn or perhaps under a tent.

Estate sales are run either by professionals or by family members. You usually will find better buys at family-run estate sales. Why? The family's knowledge of their own possessions will be slim, and their sense of value will be a sentimental one (usually a lower value) rather than a true market value. Although some seasoned dealers will only hit the "professional" estate sales because they believe that the professionals don't know it all either.

TIP: Request to be on the professional's mailing list or visit their Web site. Either attend an estate sale and ask the people running the sale if they have a mailing list or Web site, or pick up an antique journal or your local newspaper and browse through the classified section and search for "Estate Sales By [the company's name]." Sometimes preferred customers are given an early preview and buying opportunity before the public is allowed in.

As discussed in Chapter 1, at estate sales, some professionals will give out numbers in consecutive order at the sale location in advance of the scheduled opening time to control the buyer traffic. This is a favored way of doing business in Maryland and the District of Columbia because the houses or apartments are small. The number system is used primarily at estate sales where a huge crowd is expected. Remember to stand in line by 6:00 A.M. to get your number at 7:00 A.M. for the 8:00 A.M. opening. It pays to arrive early and secure a low number because the higher your number, the greater is your chances of missing good deals.

TIP: If you aren't one of the first in line but enter with the first 10 buyers, go directly to the cellar, attic, or back of the house, or better yet, bring your partner, make a plan, and divide the rooms among you.

Flea Markets

Although not technically sales, flea markets are a great place to buy and sell. Flea markets, sometimes called *swap meets,* are held all over the country. Everything is sold at flea markets from fruits, plants, and vegetables to new merchandise, crafts, and antiques. One of the most famous flea markets is called "Renningers" and consists of a farmer's market, flea market, and auction facility. Renningers is located in eastern Pennsylvania and Mount Dora, Florida (located 30 miles north of Orlando) and is open year round. Another popular flea market (and auction gallery), known as "Shipshewana," is open from May to October and is located in Indiana. Many flea markets are seasonal and often are held outdoors in a field or at a drive-in theater on a Saturday and/or a Sunday. Vendors, dealers, and other merchants set up their goods for the buying public.

Some flea markets are permanent and open all year long so that vendors can leave their booths intact. The greatest thrill about going to flea markets is that a new group of sellers or dealers may set up and sell their wares for the first time. See the Resources at the back of this book for flea market shopping locations. An example of a flea market is shown in Figure 3-4.

Garage Sale

Some people use *garage sale* generically to refer to just about any casual sale. However, careful scrutiny will prove that every garage sale is different. Some garage sales advertise only clothes. Other garage sales will have all items marked 25 cents. Most garage sales are held rain or shine because the weather is not a factor since everyone will be inside. Garage sales are a good place to pick up jewelry at reasonable prices. Most of the jewelry is thrown together in a box and usually is not sorted and displayed like at a flea market.

TIP: Keep an eye out for diamonds that get mixed in with the junk jewelry and rhinestone pieces. If you think you've found a real diamond, purchase it, and test its authenticity later. Or do a quick test on the spot. According to Helen Louth, an estate sale specialist and owner of The Hope Chest in Johnston, Rhode Island, glass will hold your breath, a diamond will not.

Figure 3-4   A country flea market is a good place to buy and sell your treasures.

Moving Sale

A moving sale is a profitable and worthwhile event because you have motivated sellers. They don't want to take a lot of items with them, so they are willing to part with items for a fair price. Sometimes families plan joint moving sales, and everyone gets into the act. Moving sales are one of the top sales to target for beginners and pros alike.

TIP: Just because a two-day moving sale is scheduled, don't rule out Sunday if you can't go on Saturday. Relatives often bring more items on the second day, especially if they have had good luck selling on the first day.

Multifamily Sale

A multifamily sale is where many families get together and hold a sale at a single location. Participants usually agree to hold the sale at one of their houses, and then everyone brings over their merchandise. Here is another great sale to attend. Why? Because you will have much more merchandise at one location and usually a greater variety of merchandise.

Neighborhood Sale

Neighborhood sales enable you to cover more ground in a short time because they usually are clustered within easy walking or driving distance of each other. If time allows, cruise through the neighborhood the day before. This will give you an advance notice of the type of neighborhood. Some neighborhoods are new, and some are old. You can make good buys at both.

The great surprise about neighborhood sales is that two neighbors could have a sale or ten neighbors could have a sale unless the sale is advertised as a "20-Family Neighborhood Sale." Always ask at the last house you visit, "Any more sales on this street?" You may run into unadvertised houses that have something you can buy and make money on when you resell. These houses may not have a great deal of traffic flow if they didn't advertise with the rest of the neighborhood. If you're a beginner, your chances of finding something first will increase because there are so many sales to target. Go to the sales that are the least crowded, or go early and be the first customer.

TIP: When you go to these sales, don't drive by sales that look unappealing or don't have much merchandise out yet. Stop at every sale in the neighborhood. All items may not be out in full view. If the neighborhood is in a large development, start at the other end of the loop, or go the opposite way of the usual traffic flow.

Pawnshops

Even though pawnshops are not technically a sale either, they are often an overlooked place to find a bargain. In the beginning days, pawnshops were a great place to sell almost any kind of merchandise for quick cash. Things were piled in, and you really had to hunt to find anything of value. Today pawnshops are brightly lighted, neatly arranged, carpeted, and piped with music. Employees behind the counter are true salespeople. Most pawnshop owners are connected to the Internet and are more market savvy than ever before. Still, in remote spots and small towns, a good pawnshop deal still exists.

Penny Sale

A penny sale or penny social, usually run by a club or organization, raises money for a specific cause. For example, a garden club could have an annual penny sale to raise money to beautify the town. A penny sale is a variation of a raffle. The items to buy are on display. You buy either an arm's length of tickets for $5 to $10 or a single ticket. A choice item such as an automobile may go as high as $1,000 for a single ticket. (Years ago the tickets sold for a penny each, hence the name *penny sale* or *penny social*.) You use your tickets to take chances on items by placing half your ticket stub (as many as you wish) in the bags or containers that corresponds with each item. At a predetermined time, a winning ticket is drawn out of the container, and the number is read aloud. The more tickets you drop in the container, the better are your chances of winning that item. Go to these sales when no other events are happening because waiting around to see if you are the winner is time-consuming.

Porch or Patio Sale

Many places have porch or patio sales instead of garage sales. These sales are sheltered, so the weather is not a factor. All items are exhibited on the porch. Often you can drive right by these sales and think someone has unloaded their summer furniture out on the porch. Often more items are for sale inside because not all pieces will fit on the porch. Pros frequently don't bother with these sales, especially if the porch sale is a continuous weekly event throughout the summer and the seller is only trying to catch new tourists passing through town.

Rummage Sale

If you love to clothes shop, this is the place to go full throttle. You can find brand-name clothing and resell those brand names for a profit. Again, condition is everything. Keep an eye out for accessories, too, including vintage top hats, bonnets, belts, scarves, shoes, and boots. Gold pins or Bakelite buttons could be the reason to buy that otherwise ordinary black jacket (in other words, the buttons might be worth more than the price of the coat). Sometimes quilts, crocheted tablecloths, and oriental rugs are hiding under used bath towels. At a designated time or near the end of a rummage sale, you can fill a bag for a dollar or two. This is when the fun begins if any good clothing outfits are left to purchase. You can make money buying and selling real fur coats, stoles, and jackets. However, some people won't sell them and some people won't buy them because of their stand on animal rights.

    The dealers hit these sales faithfully. They often wait up to an hour for the doors to open. The main reason is because rummage sales tend to have more than clothing for sale. Sometimes tables or rooms full of other donated objects are for sale at bargain prices.

TIP: When the mob is rummaging through the clothes tables and clothes racks, if the clothes look older, join the mob. Otherwise, go to the towel and accessory tables and search for rugs, linen, and jewelry.

OH! LA! LA!

A friend told me about a 1960s' vintage dress by Leonard Pucci of Paris, France, that she purchased at a rummage sale for $25. This rare, one-of-a-kind dress was signed in the cloth, "Leonard," with a black label that said, "Made in France." She sold the dress on eBay for $900.

School Sale

These sales are not usually advertised as "School Sales." Instead, watch for the name of the school in the ad, such as "Giant Yard Sale to Benefit Belmont Middle School." School sales usually are held rain or shine, unless they are held in the school parking lot, and then they will list a rain date, such as the following Saturday. This is a great sale for beginners to attend, especially if you are a parent or live in the town having the sale. You will feel good about contributing to a worthy cause by supporting your children's school fundraising activities.

TIP: Musical instruments are a specialized category. If you play an instrument or have any knowledge in this field, you could score big.

I've found cast-off musical instruments at school sales for really cheap prices because they were scratched and dented. These instruments still have value because they are usually playable, and to repair an old instrument is less expensive than buying a brand-new instrument.

Stoop Sale

In the big cities, people have stoop sales because their living space is so small, and they actually may not have a garage or a yard. The stoop is the porch or landing on a brownstone or apartment building. And often you have to stoop down to discover a hidden treasure.

Tag Sale

At a tag sale, every item should have a price tag on it. Professionals will have professional tags with the amount printed in bold. Sometimes these sales run two or three days. You may find a bargain on the second or third day as prices are slashed sometimes by 50 percent. Some tag sales have color-coded stickers, such as yellow—25 cents; red—50 cents; green—$1.00; and blue—$2.00. Here, a keen memory will serve you well, instead of having to refer to the sign and remember the prices.

TIP: If you can't remember color-coded prices, grab a pen and write a cheat sheet on the palm of your hand.

Thrift Stores

A thrift store is an accumulation of other people's donated items that are then sold through the store to profit a particular charity. A local or church-run thrift store is a better place to target than a national chain of Salvation Army or Goodwill stores. The larger, more sophisticated stores often have an expert on staff to price the items. Nowadays, if any really valuable items appear, they are sold privately or through auctions so that the organization realizes the most profit. However, it is still worth poking around thrift stores. Visit them on a regular basis because fresh merchandise comes in daily, and you may hit the big one if it's your lucky day.

Tool Sale

Buying tools, both old and new, is a profitable venture if you have any knowledge in that area. I know carpenters and plumbers who moonlight as tool dealers to make extra money on the weekends. Tool sales usually have a good listing in the ad so that you get an idea of whether they have old or slightly used (newer) tools. Sometimes a combination of old and new tools is offered. Seek out tools if they are listed among the items rather than as the main attraction. If tools are the main attraction, you will compete with knowledgeable dealers and collectors who will glean all the choice tools first.

TIP: David Capizzano, who sells under his business name Plane and Fancy Antiques, has been an avid antique carpenter tool collector since 1974. He has found many valuable tools at a fraction of their worth. David suggests that the beginner specialize in an area that she likes and learn all about that particular field. (Chapter 10 discusses specialization in depth.)

Townwide Sale

Historical societies, schools, and other groups will coordinate these sometimes-massive sales. Maps for $1 or $2 usually are handed out at a designated place and time—"Maps at 8 A.M. at the Town Hall." A town that has 50 to 100 yard sales will have plenty of merchandise. You may score big if you bring a friend because one of you can drive and the other one can read the map. You split the expenses, but you also split the profits.

SHOP 'TIL YOU DROP

"The World's Longest Yard Sale, over 450 miles on The Lookout Mountain Parkway and the U.S. 127 Corridor from Gadsden, Alabama, to Covington, Kentucky" is held every August. The event lasts nine days and spans three states. This yard sale may be worth the trip if you can coordinate sleeping quarters and a truck. For exact dates, go to www.tourdekalb.com/yardsale.

Yard Sale

This sale can run the gamut from being a small section of a person's front or back yard to every inch of their driveway, spilling out into the street. Again, check the location of the sale. Yard sales are big and small, depending on the size of the yard and the amount of merchandise. Beginners, even if you get a late start and stop at a yard sale after lunch, you may find such items as a wet suit or a snowsuit that you can list on eBay because the seasoned dealer didn't want to bother with such "new" items.

Zinnia Sale

Actually, these are few and far between, but since I have chosen to present an A to Z listing, I thought I'd end with a Z sale. Zinnias fall under the plant sale or garden club sale. Again, check the pot the plant is in and not so much the plant itself. The pot could be valuable.

MORE THAN THE PLANT WAS GREEN!

I went to a plant sale and bought a sad-looking plant for $5.00. Another buyer next to me said, "You're wasting your money. That plant isn't going to make it." I said, "Good, because I'm not much of a gardener." Often, it is better to play dumb than to give away all your secrets. Of course, I didn't buy the item for the plant; I bought the pot. Figure 3-5 shows the pot I purchased, which is a green Hampshire pottery squat vase made in Keene, New Hampshire, in the early 1900s. The vase is worth around $600. The plant has since been replaced.

Figure 3-5   Hampshire pottery vase is valued around $600.

Now that you have an understanding of different types of sales, such as auctions, eBay, garage sales, flea markets, pawnshops, and penny sales, go to one that interests you. Remember, your focus is to buy and sell and not to acquire "keepitis." If you don't know which sale to start with first, the next chapter will show you how to plot your own secret treasure map. With this map, you're bound to find a bargain before anyone else!

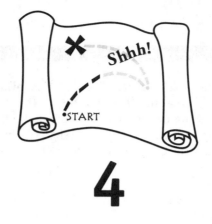

4

Creating Your Secret Treasure Map

To find great treasures at the various types of sales, you need to have a well-thought-out plan. This plan is essential if you want to arrive first and find the best buys. If detailed map plotting seems tedious, stick to it because this process gets easier with experience. I've found numerous treasures because I diligently plotted my map each week. This chapter covers how to plot your own garage and yard sale routes from the listings or directory in the newspaper. You will find garage sales listed in other places as well, and you can add these sales to your map as well.

TRACKING DOWN GARAGE SALE ADVERTISEMENTS

As you focus on buying at garage sales, you will see advertisements everywhere. Ads are in newspapers, in weekly shoppers, on bulletin boards, on the radio, on the Internet, on telephone poles, and at intersections. Let's briefly examine the places where you might find garage sale ads.

Print Advertisements

As discussed in Chapter 1, the newspaper is your best source to find advertised sales. Every newspaper in the country usually has one issue (one day of the week) that features the majority of its garage/yard sale classified ads. It's typically the Thursday or Friday edition (in anticipation of weekend sales); if you are unsure of the day, call the paper and ask. When that edition comes out, buy it. All sale announcements or ads usually are located in the classified sections under the heading "Yard Sales" or "Garage Sales."

Buy both your local weekly and daily papers (usually a Friday paper for Saturday sales). These papers have a "What's Happening" section that lists craft fairs, white elephant sales, book sales, and so on by date and time. Other sections of the paper such as the "Bargain Bin" or the "Community Bulletin Board" will list upcoming events that may include a school sale or church bazaar. Other print media include school newsletters, library and church bulletins, and fraternal and civic organization newsletters.

TIP: Check all sections of your local paper, not just the classified, and cross-reference the sales.

Media Advertisements

Listen to radio announcements. Watch the local cable network for weekend activities in your area. Go on the Internet and type in "Garage Sales" or "Yard Sales" to find sale listings all over the country. Call the chamber of commerce in a town you want to target.

Posters and Other Signs

Garage sales are also advertised on drive-by signs at schools, churches, and community buildings. Grocery stores and post offices also list upcoming events, garage sales, and items for sale on their bulletin boards. Brightly colored posters and cardboard signs are posted at intersections and on telephone poles.

PRIORITIZE THE SALES TO ATTEND

In the spring, when yard sales bloom like daffodils, how do you decide which one to go to first? What if the newspaper lists 2 estate sales, a multifamily sale, a townwide sale, 7 yard sales, 10 garage sales, and a 20-neighborhood sale all scheduled for the same Saturday and within a 40-mile radius? What do you do? Close your eyes and randomly pick one? No, you should have a strategy, and I'm going to teach you how to read an ad and prioritize the sales to attend. This is a time-consuming task, but the payoff is worth the effort.

For example, suppose that the following sale is advertised in the paper. This is the only estate sale that day. Please read the ad, and then answer the questions. Circle Y for yes and N for no.

Estate Sale—Brookline, Sat. & Sun. 11/1 & 11/2 at 8 A.M. Contents of house and garage, some antiques. 200 Poor Farm Road. No Early Birds!

1. Would you go to this sale?   Y or N
2. Would you go to this sale first?   Y or N

3. Would you go even though the ad says, "some antiques"?   Y or N
    4. Would you go to this sale if it rains?   Y or N
    5. Would you go early if the sign says, "No Early Birds?"   Y or N

If you answered, "Yes" to every question, you're right. Here are the answers and why:

    1. Yes. You'd go to this sale because at an estate sale, usually everything is for sale.
    2. Yes. You'd go to this sale first because family heirlooms could surface. You have the best chance of finding collectibles when an entire house is being sold.
    3. Yes. You'd go because the ad states "some antiques," signifying that "some" could be many or only a few.
    4. Yes. If it rains, you'd go to the sale because most estate sales are held in the house, so weather is not a factor.
    5. Yes. You would arrive at 6:00 a.m. even though the ad says, "No Early Birds!" There will be other early birds besides you. Either the seller will let you in, or you will wait for two hours on his doorstep to get in first.

Once you read through the ads and become familiar with the sales, you need to dissect the ads, underline key words, and plot your map.

TIP: Steve Gass, a garage sale aficionado from Connecticut, always gives priority to a two-day sale, especially an estate sale. He says the sellers are usually first-timers because they think they have enough merchandise for two days. Steve says the sellers don't realize that all the valuable merchandise goes on the first day, and often, only the junk is left on the second day.

TEN STEPS TO PLOT YOUR TREASURE MAP

Once you've read the ads, it's time for action. To make the best use of your time, you need to have a plan. Since this is a search for valuable goods, I call my plan a treasure map. On this map you're going to plot all the sales you want to shop and the best route to take. Your newspaper clipping is your map key. It is important to mark up your copy and underline trigger words and abbreviate headers to give you a quick, easy reference at a glance. Thorough map plotting in the spring or fall will take about an hour because the sales are so numerous. This map is one way to stay ahead of competitive buyers.

A FREE RIDE!

Joan's vacation trip was practically free last year because she found an eighteenth-century candle stand at a tag sale (see Figure 4-1). In colonial days, people read by candlelight. A candle was placed on a stand—thus the name candle stand. The stand that Joan found was used as a plant stand. However, she immediately recognized the shape of the legs, known as a "snake foot."

Step 1: Clip the Garage/Yard Sale Listing or Directory from the Newspaper

If you live in an urban area or in a community serviced by more than one paper, buy each edition on its strongest listings day. Many people have yard sales at the last minute, especially if the weekend weather forecast is in their favor. They often miss the weekly deadline to advertise their garage sale, so that's why the daily paper is a good place to double-check locations. The deadlines on a daily paper are only a few days rather than a week. The seller may have thrown a quick ad in the daily paper to catch buyers who are visiting from out of town.

Figure 4-1 A cherry candle stand used as a plant stand and purchased for $10 at an estate sale sold for $800 at a country auction.

TIP: Look at garage/yard sale listings when on vacation because you never know when or where you'll find a treasure.

Step 2: Copy the Garage/Yard Sale Listing or Directory

Once you've cut out the yard sale listing, photocopy it. Surrounding towns are listed in the ad, but concentrate on the town with the most sales, in this case Milford (see Figure 4-2). On your copy, cross off all the towns you're not going to target. Circle any sales that are advertised for the following weekend, and put those on your calendar for next week's map plotting. The figure shows only the towns you're going to target. The other towns are crossed off, except Mont Vernon, which is on route to Milford. If you plan to go only on Saturday, cross off other days, such as Thursday, Friday, and Sunday, so that you don't get confused.

TIP: Make several copies of towns within a 40-mile radius of your starting point, and keep them in a file. If you don't have a copy machine, go to an office supply store or use an erasable map.

Step 3: Copy the Town Map

Now that you've targeted Milford, copy the town street map plus any other town(s) en route, such as Mont Vernon (see Figure 4-3). You may have to reduce the map size when you make a copy. Just make sure that you can read the street names in the smaller print.

Step 4: Search the Ads for Outstanding Sales

Outstanding sales are estate sales, a 10-or-more-neighborhood sales, and 50- to 100-family or townwide sales. If a townwide sale is two hours away, it's worth the trip. Whichever sale you choose to attend first, remember to arrive early. The best feature about a townwide sale is that the road map is already completed for you. To obtain a map and address locations in the area, you will have to pay a small fee at designated location (such as the town hall) at a certain time (say, 8:00 A.M.).

TIP: At a townwide sale, don't wait until the 8:00 A.M. start time. Go earlier, and visit as many sales as you can, and then buy a map to locate the sales you missed. By 8:00 A.M., most of the sales have been picked over by dealers anyway.

Figure 4-2   On your yard sale directory, cross off the towns you will not target.
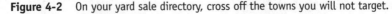

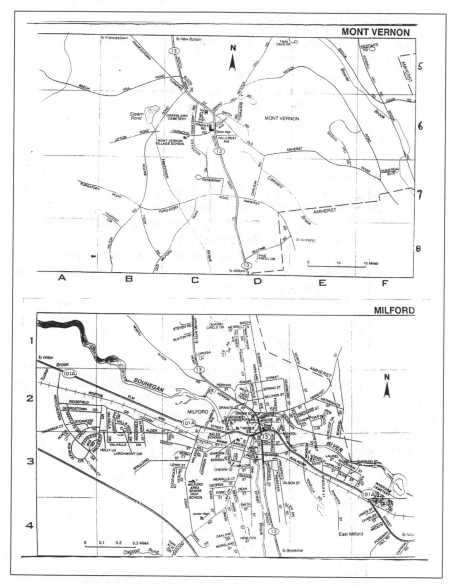

Figure 4-3   Copy the maps of the towns you will target.

Step 5: Underline the Key Words in the Ad

Does the ad mention any items that you specialize in, such as dolls, rugs, military items, fishing equipment, or musical instruments? Are you interested only in furniture, tools, books, or jewelry? Underline those words in the ad. Does the ad list baby clothes, CDs, videos, and kids' toys? Underline the items that you think you can buy and resell for a profit.

Is your focus antiques? Identify where the word *antique* appears in the ad and who is holding the sale.

- If *antique* is part of the title, such as "John's Antique Shop is reducing its inventory—Big Sale," put that sale at the end of your list. The dealer may only want to sell off stagnant stock.
- If you read further and discover that John has died and that the shop has to close, then target that sale as one of your top five.
- If the word *antique* is within the body of the ad, then target that sale also. For example, if the ad says, "Garage Sale—some antiques, furniture, household, tools," definitely rank this sale as a "must go to" on your list.

Step 6: Red Pen the Sale Type on the Directory

Underline the sale type in the headline or body of the ad. Use a one- or two-letter abbreviation of the sale header, and write these abbreviations in the margins. For example, mark an A for antiques, an ES for estate sale, G for garage sale, MF for multifamily sale, MO for moving sale, N for neighborhood sale, O for office sale, R for rummage sale, and Y for yard sale. If you plan to target two or more towns, mark those other towns with three abbreviated letters and circle them, such as MTV for Mont Vernon.

Step 7: Locate the Roads on the Map

Do this step to help you decide the direction in which you're going to travel first. (I promise it won't be in circles.)

1. Locate the streets on the map using the alphabetical streets and coordinates in the map key (i.e., Secomb Road, D8), and with a highlighter, underline the road. (For illustration purposes in this book, the targeted streets are marked with a series of X's.)
2. Next, use a blue pen (or other standout color) to write down the street address or house number of the sale near the located road on your map. Refer to your yard sale directory. Sometimes a number is not given, only a street name, so you have to guess.

TIP: Often a church will not list a street address; keep the phone book handy, and call if the complete address is not advertised in the newspaper. Or if you find that the street is really long, call a business on that street to ask its street number to help you pinpoint the sale location.

Step 8: Transfer the Sale Type and Start Time from the Directory to the Map

For the map to be useful at a glance, you need to list key features, such as the sale type and the start time. Most sales start at either 8:00 or 9:00 A.M. If a sale starts earlier, put an asterisk (*) near the time. Target these early sales, especially the ones that start at 6:30 or 7:00 A.M. And plan to arrive at these sales at 5:30 A.M. Are you willing to get up and go on a Saturday morning when the rest of the family is sleeping? Try it a few times. The first couple of excursions are fun and exciting. After a few trips, however, you may discover that buying at garage sales is a once-a-year event and not a weekend mission. You could return empty handed. At auctions or antique shops, you usually don't have to hunt before dawn.

Step 9: Rank the Sales

To plot the route you're going to take on Saturday morning, you need to rank, or number, the sales in Milford in the order in which you plan to stop at them. This is where a close read of the classified ads will prove important. By looking at your directory and coordinating it with your map plotting, you'll devise the best route to follow. The number 1 sale is the sale you like the best or the sale that has the earliest start time. However, you may find an unadvertised sale on the way and stop there first. Number and circle the sales in preference order.

Besides estate and townwide sales, I always give priority to multifamily sales, moving sales, and neighborhood sales. Your map is a guide, and the route is not written in stone. Flexibility is the key. This is why it's important to know the start time and location of each sale. Figure 4-4 shows the map in its final numbered order.

TIP: A garage sale preference also is based on street and neighborhood location. With experience, you will know what parts of town seem to have the better merchandise.

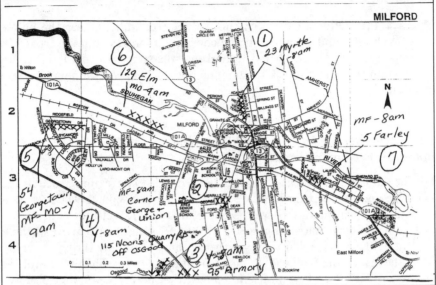

Figure 4-4   This is your completed treasure map for quick and easy bargain shopping.

Step 10: Number the Ads on the Directory as You Did on the Map

The reason to coordinate ad and map numbers is for a quick reference. (Glance at number 1 on the map and refer to number 1 on the directory.) This will come in handy if you get lost, misread an ad, or want to quickly reread a description. Number and circle the order of the sale on the directory as you did on the map (see Figure 4-5). Note: If another town has a number of sales and you want to plot them alongside the main town that you're targeting, use letters such as A, B, C, and so on, and circle them.

LET THE TREASURE HUNT BEGIN

Once your map is completed, you can see clearly which sales are within a few streets of each other. You may not have known this unless you had plotted your map. Other sales may have miles between them. Focus on any sale clusters to increase your chances of finding more treasures and more sales in less time. When your map is completed, put it in your car. When Saturday morning arrives, you will have a head start on the competition.

My final word of advice is to have some kind of plan. I've given you one plan (the treasure map) to get you organized and on your way. Others

Figure 4-5 Your preference order on the yard sale directory corresponds with the numbered order on your map.

will have a different strategy and game plan. Still others will "wing it" and have no map or plan to their garage sale treasure hunting. Find a plan that works for you. The race is on. Everyone is looking for that ultimate bargain. Are you going to find it first? Following your secret treasure map certainly will help.

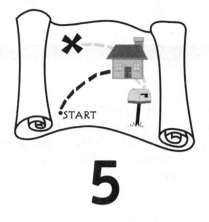

5

Treasure Hunting in Your Own Backyard

The community which you currently live in or which you grew up in is a valuable resource when you start to buy and sell. Do you know any community personnel, or are one yourself, or do you belong to any clubs in town? These people in the inner circle may give you important information about someone in town. Also, anyone in the trade or service industry gains trust with their customers and has access to people's home and their contents.

THE BUTCHER, THE BAKER, THE CANDLESTICK MAKER

The following people (or others) may open up another channel through which you can purchase items to resell: (*Note:* A nice gesture is to compensate these people for their information or to split the proceeds if you find a chest filled with treasures.)

Attorney

Search out an attorney who handles wills, probate, and estate settlements. Often, when people die, an appraiser or antique dealer is called on to give a fair market value appraisal before the estate can be dispersed or liquidated. Let the attorney know that you're in the business of liquidating both single items and entire estates. Certain attorneys just specialize in estate settlement. Check online or in the Yellow Pages if you don't know any attorneys personally.

> **TIP:** Paralegals usually handle a majority of the legwork in busy law firms, and you may find it easier to make an appointment with a paralegal to talk about your services than with an attorney.

Banker

Bankers are often executors of estates and have business relationships with antique dealers, appraisers, and auctioneers. Get to know the bankers in the trust department of your local bank who specialize in estate planning. See if you can give a 10-minute presentation about your services. Include moving, shipping items to heirs, selling any items not wanted by relatives, and leaving the property "broom clean."

 TIP: Find out what other companies are charging for their services, and offer a discount or a lower percentage just to get your foot in the door.

Barber

The barber knows all the locals in town, especially if the community is small. He knows whose mother died, what great aunt is in a nursing home, and which son is going to inherit his grandfather's farm.

Bartender

This person usually gets the scoop, good or bad, on family situations—a divorce in the works, a person who has lost her job, or a single mom raising her kids. All these people may want to sell items because they need to pay their bills. You can go in and offer them a fair price for their possessions.

Chauffeur

If you are a chauffeur or know one, you may find merchandise in other states or out in the country when you drive to the summer cottage on the

FARBER THE BARBER

A country barber from Idaho used to cut hair for a living until he discovered a more profitable way to make a day's pay. Customers willingly told him about personal property they were trying to dispose of and asked him if he knew anyone they could contact. At first, Farber told them about a local auctioneer, and then after several years, Farber got smart and bought and sold all the merchandise himself.

lake or take a trip to the penthouse in the city. A young man I knew had a summer job as a chauffeur and traveled from Boston, Massachusetts, to North Conway, New Hampshire, every weekend. The woman he chauffeured loved to go antiquing. He learned a lot from her and developed his own interest in stoneware jugs and baskets. He built up quite a collection and later sold off part of his collection when he needed the money for graduate school.

Dump Attendant

At one time and in some small communities even today, the dump attendant has rights to anything that is brought to the town dump. If the dump attendant doesn't want these items, he will place them in a free room for the public to rummage through if they need something. Many people have picked the dump and sold things that look like junk for a great profit.

TIP: Pay the local dump attendant a set fee for the month to hold out anything that is not damaged or broken too badly, including furniture, china, glass, pottery, and so on. On top of the monthly fee, pay him for the items that he sets aside for you.

Funeral Director

Ask the funeral director if you can place your business card or pamphlet on one of the tables or display racks at the funeral home. Often, when relatives of the deceased are from out of town and funeral arrangements have been made locally, they also search for someone who can settle the estate.

ONE PERSON'S TRASH IS
ANOTHER PERSON'S TREASURE

Maurice volunteered at a dumpsite two days a week for years. He had first rights to anything that came into the dump. His best deal was a truckload of heavy iron pieces that the owners did not want on their property anymore. Maurice gladly hauled the junk to his home, where later, since he knew the "junk" to be a blacksmith shop in its entirety, he sold it to a private collector for over $10,000.

Furnace Technician

This person usually has access to cellars. A wide variety of old things are stored and tucked away in cellars. Most technicians aren't going to actually "case the joint." They might see a pile of "junk" stacked in the corner and make a comment to you if they know that you buy and sell used merchandise. The technician should inquire first with the owner to see if she will give the technician permission to reveal her name. Then see if you can contact the owners in case they want to sell that old rickety red table or decorated stoneware (see Figure 5-1) or other items that are no longer providing any function other than collecting dust.

Garbage Collector

Much like a dump attendant, a garbage collector gets to see all the unwanted trash. If the garbage collector has an eye for the old and valuable or learns how to sort treasures from trash, he can start a good second-hand business. A man from Rhode Island started this way. He filled his sheds and barns so full of salable merchandise from the curbside trash that he became an auctioneer so that he could sell off everything. He so enjoyed the process and the extra money that he gave up his garbage route and went into the antique and auction business full time.

Figure 5-1   Stoneware crocks such as these, found in a cellar, are worth hundreds of dollars to specialized collectors.

TIP: A great way to make extra money is to sell scrap at the scrap yard. You can scrap copper, brass, and aluminum pieces to a "scrapper," who gives you money based on weight (currently 40 to 60 cents a pound). The scrapper then smelts down the scrap and, in turn, sells the recycled material to manufacturing companies.

Handyman/Housekeeper

These people are trusted employees around the house, both inside and outside. They may have access to garages, barns, storage sheds, and other rooms or areas in a house where a few inquiries could result in a few treasures.

Hairdresser

No secrets are kept from the local hairdresser. The hairdresser, like the barber, is a great source of private and personal information. The hairdresser knows everyone's dilemmas and crises. The hairdresser knows whether someone has to move suddenly or someone becomes ill and the relatives have to dispose of all the personal belongings. Ask if you can leave your business card on the counter and/or if the hairdresser will give his clients your name.

Mail Carrier

Some mail carriers take the mail directly up to a house or apartment. The carrier gets to know the inhabitants and their life histories, including interests, hobbies, and collecting habits. Over time, the residents trust the mail carrier and his recommendations. The mail carrier could recommend that you visit Mildred over on the lake because she wants to get rid of some trinkets.

IN RAIN, SLEET, AND SNOW

In inclement weather, Sam, a mail carrier, often hand delivers the mail to the elderly. His elderly customers appreciate this service. Over the years, they have discovered that Sam is an avid collector of old radios. Sam will buy old radios from his customers, fix them up, keep the best ones, and sell the others on eBay.

Plumber

Plumbers visit the bathrooms (sometimes on multiple levels of a house), kitchens, and basements to deal with leaking pipes. They are a good source of knowledge as to the types of furnishings in the homes they service. I know a father and son in the plumbing business who have a successful side business buying and selling old and discarded plumbing equipment. They sell the discarded equipment to other homeowners who need starter or old-style fixtures.

Postmaster

The postmaster, especially in small towns, is on a first-name basis with most of the people who come into the post office. The postmaster knows when people are moving or changing occupations, who's coming into town, when their next operation is scheduled, how many kids they have, and usually most of their life histories.

Real Estate Agent

Get to know the real estate agents or brokers in your town. Tell them that you are in the business of buying and selling general household and antique merchandise. If they give you a successful lead, you can repay them in the form of a finder's fee. Many agents are willing to do this because they have access to a house first, and the sellers want to know who they can contact to dispose of their personal property.

Visiting Nurse

This person often takes care of elderly or sick people. Younger relatives may arrive in town to check on the elderly person. Often the relatives have to decide what to do with accumulated belongings. The nurse could discreetly recommend your name as a liquidator.

FLY BY DAY OR NIGHT

Another way to know your community and the sales that are scheduled for a particular weekend is to do a drive-by or a "practice run" the day or night before the sales. Go to every sale you've plotted on your map because you may change your route when you do a drive-by. Some people will post signs the night before, and you can easily follow the signs to their house.

Here are some things to look for when you do your drive-by that might persuade you to stop at one sale over another one. Make sure that you stop at a sale or plan to attend an auction if you see any of the following clues:

1. The architecture of the house is old, that is, salt box style, cape, or colonial, because the personal property inside could include antiques.
2. The grass is uncut, the hedges aren't trimmed, or the house needs painting. Perhaps no one has lived there for a while, and you may find some good deals as relatives dispose of items that have been left in the house or around the property.
3. Laundry is hanging out on a clothesline. Notice what type of laundry. Is the clothing from an older generation? This may signify that old items or antiques may be offered at the sale. See Figure 5-2.
4. Apple trees, lilac bushes, or hydrangeas are on the property. This suggests that the property is old, and valuable items could be inside.
5. The mail is overflowing in the mailbox. This indicates that the owner has moved or is deceased, and an estate sale may be planned.
6. Out-of-state cars are parked in the driveway. This suggests that relatives are in town to settle the estate or contents and may not know what items are worth.
7. The porch has furniture on it. Old porch furniture could indicate old or antique items inside as well.

Figure 5-2 Look for laundry on the line if you drive by a home the day before a sale. If the clothing (and the house) is from an older time period, place an asterisk (*) near this sale because you will want to include it on your yard sale route.

8. A dumpster is on the property. This suggests that the owner is moving or that an older home is being cleaned out. Sometimes trash in the dumpster is money in your pocket.

TIP: A dumpster is an often overlooked place to search for treasures. A man named Dan from Minnesota earned a reputation and became known as "Dumpster Dan" because he would go "dumpster diving" and find all kinds of free items that he could sell to others, including working TVs, furniture, golf clubs, sets of dishes, toys, and so on.

EAST SIDE, WEST SIDE

Is the east side or west side of the city more apt to have deals and better antiques or barely used furniture and household goods? Focus on which areas to go to for the best estate, yard, or garage sales. Over time, through trial and error, you'll know which sections of town to target first.

Also find out when the town or city has spring and/or fall cleanup day. This usually occurs one weekend in the spring or fall when residents can leave big pieces of furniture, lawn equipment, toys, bikes, and so on at curbside without paying any money to have them hauled away by the town. Ride around in your truck for several nights before cleanup day, and fill your truck with salable items. You'll be amazed at what people throw out and what you can pick up for free and resell for a decent amount of money. Figure 5-3 shows the kinds of treasures you can find at the curb.

A DATE TO REMEMBER!

Several couples I know look forward to the annual cleanup day in their town. They spend an evening and drive around town to collect other people's trash intended for the dump. Jeffrey says that cleanup day is so popular that a traffic jam occurs in front of his house and extends for five miles. Rather than getting stuck in the long line, Jeffrey and his wife, Kim, start "picking" the curbside before rush hour. They've found desks, TVs, toys, gym equipment, tools, and kitchen appliances. Their best find was a very expensive wooden swing set in perfect condition. Each year they fill their van four or five times with free merchandise, and several weeks later they have their own yard sale and make money.

Figure 5-3 Treasures abound at curbside during town cleanup days.

NOW YOU KNOW!

So now you might want to join that local garden, land conservation, or Rotary club. When you conduct your business in town, don't hurry. Talk with the postmaster, strike up a conversation with the guys at the dump, and visit the barber or hairdresser a little more often. Go to town meetings and local fundraisers. There's truth in the saying, "It's not what you know, but whom you know." Knowing your community may create a profitable relationship that will endure for many years.

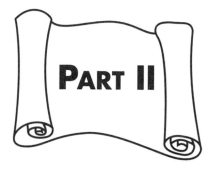

PART II

THE BASICS OF BUYING

(Photo courtesy of Gems of New England.)

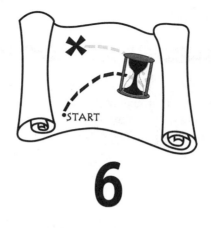

6

Finding the Bargains Fast!

You've arrived at a sale, a show, or a flea market. Now what? Every sale is
different but for one point: The start-to-finish race is the same—*fast.* The
adage "Time is of the essence" is certainly true. Each event is like a sprint, and
each sale day is like a track meet. Ed Correia, a dealer who sells at antique
shows throughout New England, calls these early birds the "runners" because
they literally run from one booth to another searching for hidden treasures.

For fun, you might want to see how many sales you can attend and how
much you can buy in the shortest amount of time. You're in a race against
time, the elements, and the competition. And your heart races, too, sending
your adrenaline into overdrive. Racing from sale to sale is a real high and, for
some, an addiction. *Caution:* If you experience any of these symptoms, you're
well on your way to becoming a garage sale "junkie" or a flea market fanatic.

WHAT SHOULD I BUY?

To find those hidden treasures faster than everyone else, you need to know
what to buy. In general, buy

- *Old (antique).* These items are more valuable, and you will make a
  higher return on your investment.
- *New (or barely used).* These items will be cheaper to buy than if you
  purchased them at a retail store. You can resell them at a lower price
  than a retail store and still make a profit.
- *Both old and new.* Don't limit yourself to buying just old or new when
  there's money to be made in both.
- *One category, for example, old teddy bears.* This is known as *specializing.* See Chapter 10 for more details.

Go to a flea market and look for one particular category that interests you, you will be able to scan through each booth faster than the person looking for general merchandise. For example, if you love bears, buy an old teddy bear. An old teddy bear may have one of or all the features you should look for, such as

- Straw-filled
- Humpback
- Glass eyes
- Original tag

Does the bear have a button in its ear and a tag or label that says, "Steiff"? This bear is more valuable. Remember, condition is everything. Figure 6-1 shows an old teddy bear.

CHOOSING THE CORRECT SIGN

So you have your map in hand, but what happens when you see a sale advertised on a telephone pole that isn't plotted on your map, or you're on vacation and don't have a map. Can you simply follow the signs to a garage sale?

Figure 6-1 This German humpback teddy bear from the 1890s is worth $300 to $500.

Tracking down a sale is often a time-consuming process that literally could have you going in circles, not to mention the gas and mileage you waste while getting lost. Here's why some signs will drive you nuts:

- The lettering is so small or illegible that you actually have to park your car, get out, and read the location of the sale.
- Old signs often are posted on utility poles along with new signs. Old signs are faded, water stained, curled up, or have a prior date listed.
- Some signs have no date or start time, such as "Sat. 8 A.M."
- Directional arrows are somehow forgotten on a sign. If you're new to an area or just passing through and don't have a local map, you probably won't find the sale.
- Some signs don't list the street number, such as number 34, or the street name, such as Brook Lane.
- You follow one color sign, and it changes from pink to green, so you don't know if the sign you started following is for the same sale at which you will end up.
- Some sales are three to four miles down a back road. Distance is not usually given on a sign. In the rare case that it is posted, you will have to decide if the five-mile trip is worth your time or if that sale draws you too far out of the mainstream of other sales.

Figure 6-2 shows an intersection with a number of sale signs. Which one would you follow?

TIP: Following signs to auctions sometimes will test your patience as well, especially if the sales are held in an unfamiliar location and the directions aren't explicit.

THE DISPOSABLE SIGN

Once, when traveling through a city, I followed signs to an estate sale. I followed the sign into the dumpster that was on the property! No one was around, and from the looks of the dumpster, the remnants of the sale were obvious—nothing but trash left. The estate sale had already happened, probably last weekend, but the owner had failed to take down the signs. I did look in the dumpster but found nothing of value.

Figure 6-2 So many signs, so little time. To save time, choose the sign that gives the most information if the sale is not plotted on your treasure map.

TEN TIPS TO CASE THE JOINT FAST!

When it comes to staying ahead of your competition, there are 10 tips that will aid you in your search for valuable treasures in the shortest amount of time. Aim for one minute or less at each garage sale or flea market vendor (unless, of course, you find something amazing). If you make a purchase, an average amount of time to spend is five minutes. If you're targeting an estate sale, you'll have to readjust your time because looking through a house will take longer.

1. Refer to Your Treasure Map

For garage sales, follow your first target on your treasure map. Watch for signs posted on telephone poles. Follow the signs that are the same color; the same color is usually for the same yard sale, but not always. At a neighborhood sale, stop at the first house that has its garage open. Furniture and miscellaneous items also may be lined up on the driveway. Glance up the road to see if more houses have merchandise on their lawns.

For flea markets or shows, target new vendors or the average person selling items from his house instead of going to the regular dealers first. Some flea markets and shows have maps available with vendor locations.

2. Position Your Vehicle

For garage sales, position your car or van on the right side of the street just a few feet beyond the targeted house. This will prevent you from getting blocked in if the sale is invaded by others. In addition, you're also headed in the right direction for the next sale in the neighborhood. Evaluate whether or not it is advantageous to park in the middle of the neighborhood and walk to each sale or drive to each one. In a short time, other cars will surround you, making it impossible for you to leave when you're done. You don't want to get blocked in and have to wait 10 minutes for another buyer to move a truck. That consumes valuable minutes that could cause you to miss good deals at other sales. Figure 6-3 shows you the parking jam to avoid at a sale.

For flea markets or shows, park in designated parking areas (you may have to pay a parking fee), and park as close as you can to the action. If you purchase a lot of items, you won't have as far to walk to your car. If you buy furniture, you are often allowed to drive between the rows of vendors to load your purchases.

3. Scope Out the Seller

At a multiseller sale, as you inspect items, notice how many sellers are present. You may have to pay each seller before you move on to the next table. This is

Figure 6-3 A typical buying frenzy at this yard sale has resulted in jammed parking. A quick getaway is impossible unless you have parked your car strategically.

how flea markets and shows work, also. Ask any pertinent questions, negotiate a price, pay for your merchandise, make a quick getaway, and go on to the next seller.

When you're at a yard sale, notice if the seller is still unloading items out of the house or car. Often, hanging around a few more minutes to poke through boxes that no one else has looked in is worth your time. Or ask if the person has any more furniture in the house that she couldn't move outside because of inclement weather or lack of help. Sometimes people have signs to a post that say, "More furniture inside," or "Bedroom set upstairs—$250."

4. Scan the Merchandise

On arrival at a garage sale, flea market, or show, scan the merchandise. If you have a partner, you and your partner will cover more sales in less time than a buyer going solo.

Are you interested in furniture? Make a quick assessment of any of the pieces and the price on each item.

- Are any drawers missing?
- Is the top split or badly scratched?
- Are any handles missing off the front?
- Have any handles been replaced?
- Are all the legs on the table?
- Does the chair have all its spindles?
- Is the seat in good condition?
- Is the price in my ballpark or out in left field?

Are you interested in collectibles or small items such as china or glass? Scan the tables and boxes, and ask yourself these questions:

- Do any items have chips or cracks?
- Has the item been repaired?
- Is the set complete?
- Is the item a reproduction? (More on this later.)
- Can I make my profit even if the item is damaged?
- Are any pieces signed or marked on the bottom?

I've seen experienced buyers and dealers do the "once-over" in 10 seconds and leave for the next sale. Other seasoned buyers and dealers do yard sale drive-bys without getting out of their vehicle. This takes a trained eye. I almost always stop, get out, and do an on-site scan. I need the exercise, and my goal of finding that special something compels me to look in every box.

TIP: Make up a code between yourself and your partner so that you can grab something fast before someone else gets it. For example, if you see jewelry on a table, and your partner is nearer to the jewelry than you are, yell out, "Look, there's Ruby." Your partner will know to scan the tables for jewelry.

5. Grab Hold of the Merchandise

As if a big tornado is bearing down on you, grab hold of anything you think you're interested in before the treasure flies away or is scooped up by someone else. Without a moment to lose, do the following:

- Pick up that item you think has resale value and put it in your bag. You can decide later if you don't want it.
- If an item doesn't have a price tag, scoop it up anyway. You can ask about the price when the seller is unoccupied with other customers.
- If you're unsure whether you want an item because the price is high, pick it up. You don't want to say to yourself later, "Oh, I should have bought that."
- If you see a piece of furniture that you want to buy, immediately tell the owner, take the price tag off the item, or put your own "sold" sticker on it.

STICKLEY FURNITURE WORTH THE GAMBLE

The Arts and Crafts Movement (of the late nineteenth and early twentieth centuries) exemplified oak furniture that was simple and durable and became known as "mission furniture" or "furniture with a purpose." The most well-known craftsman of the period was Gustav Stickley of Eastwood, New York. Stickley's trademark was a red decal with a joiner's compass and the motto, "Als ik kan" (As I can). When Gustav went bankrupt in 1915, his brothers, Leopold and J. George Stickley, bought his factory. The brothers made furniture under the name of Stickley Manufacturing Company, Inc., and signed their pieces as L. & J. G. Stickley. George and Albert started the Stickley Brothers Company in Grand Rapids, Michigan.

If you see something that is valuable, alert the seller that you want that item, especially if you just found a Stickley server for $100; then you've made your profit for the next few months. You will want to buy and load that item immediately. Stickley furniture is worth thousands of dollars. Figure 6-4 shows an example of Stickley furniture.

TIP: If you buy a piece of furniture, such as a bureau, and have to return to the sale later to pick it up, always take a drawer or two with you. That way you are assured that no one else will want your item. It also can prevent the seller from accidentally selling the piece twice.

6. Give the Merchandise a Second Look

You may miss something on the first scan because you went too fast. Second looks are opportunities to dig a little deeper into boxes, to look more closely at the stack of books, to see if any of the glassware is signed or damaged, or grab any gold pieces mixed in among the junk jewelry. Now's the time to read through the titles of books or flip through the pictures you saw on the way in. But again, I have to emphasize you need to do this quickly and efficiently.

On my second sweep through a stack of pictures, I found a miniature interior bedroom scene with three colonial women. Scrawled in pencil in the

Figure 6-4   Stickley furniture is a definite treasure to find at a garage sale. If you see something that has this boxy style, tell the seller you want to buy it or place your own "sold" tag on the item before anyone else does.

lower right was the artist's signature, "Wallace Nutting" (see Figure 6-5). Even if you know nothing about Wallace Nutting, you would purchase that print for 25 cents, right?

7. Haggle Quickly

After you've found something that you want to buy, find the seller and ask, "Is that your best price?" Sometimes, the seller may take off more than you expect. Of course, if you arrive at a sale at 6 A.M. and ask that question (and you should), the seller may laugh at you and say, "I'm not ready yet, or it's a little too early; come back this afternoon." Then you have to decide if you're going to pay full price or put the item back on the table. No matter what, if you're going to bargain, do so quickly. The key here is to ask for a reduction on the price, but don't get into a long conversation about Grandma's life story. Chapter 7 gives you tips on how to haggle with the seller.

8. Ask the Magic Question

Always ask sellers if they have any more items for sale. If a couple is running the sale, ask each of them separately, "Are you bringing any more items out?" Often, one of them will say, "Oh, yes, wait a minute; I forgot to bring out the

Figure 6-5   Miniature interior print by Wallace Nutting, worth around $200.

WALLACE NUTTING PRINTS ARE A FAVORITE FIND

Wallace Nutting was a clergyman, furniture maker, writer, and photographer who lived in New England in the early 1900s. He traveled all over the world, published 20 books, reproduced American furniture, and took 50,000 photographs. Of all his photographic work, Nutting is best known for his interior and exterior prints of New England. His interior colonial scenes and scenes of children are more valuable and sought after by collectors. His prints, which are, in reality, hand-colored photographs, have sold from hundreds to thousands of dollars. A collection of his furniture, prints, and books is on permanent exhibition at the Wadsworth Atheneum in Hartford, Connecticut.

box of old silver." If it's early in the day, the merchandise may be wrapped up in a box somewhere. In that case, you might hear the seller say, "Oh, I brought those dishes out. They're in a box somewhere."

9. Quickly Pay for Your Goods

Gather your items together and pay the cashier. At some sales, the cashier is not the owner, so make sure that the prices are marked. If a price is not marked, the seller will call out to the cashier the amount you agreed on. At a flea market or show, if the owner is on a break and someone else is filling in, you may have to return later to get a better deal. Have the attendant put the item aside for you.

Try to have the exact change; that way you can square up and keep moving. If you don't have the exact change but are willing to give up a few cents to gain precious time, don't wait for the change.

10. The Getaway

At garage sales, quickly take your purchases to the car. Take the extra 10 seconds to wrap up fragile merchandise. Move the box to the back of the car, nearest your seat, so that you have more room to load more boxes or anything big. Move things around now rather than waiting until you can't move anything. You will lose storage space because you didn't pack purchases tightly together in the beginning. If your tote bag is full, empty the bag or carry more than one bag so that you have something to load up again at the next sale.

At flea markets, don't keep running back and forth to load your purchases. You will lose valuable time. Have several shopping bags with you or a backpack. If the item is heavy, pay for the item, get a receipt, and ask the vendor to hold the item until you can pick it up.

Remember, aim for a total shopping time of one minute per vendor or garage sale. Then take a deep breath and a sip of your water. Get energized with a snack. You're ready to hit the next sale. You still have to drive to 20 more yard sales or sprint past 80 more flea market vendors. Hurry! The race is on. The clock is ticking. The bell is about to ring. Will you win the prize? If you can wheel and deal with a seller, you may get a big prize for less money. The next chapter tells you how.

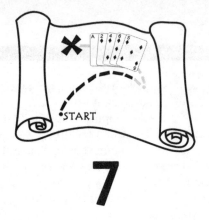

7

Wheeling and Dealing

When it comes to garage sales, estate sales, and all other kinds of sales, everything is negotiable, so bargain, bargain, bargain! This is the attitude that will get you some good deals. Other terms used interchangeably with the word *bargain* are

- *Dicker*
- *Haggle*
- *Wheel and deal*

You can bargain when you attend garage sales, flea markets, pawnshops, and shows. As a buyer, you always haggle for the best price (which is often the lowest). To some extent, you haggle at an auction. When the auctioneer asks for $50, you can bid $25. Of course, the bid may exceed $100 but maybe not.

If you're already in sales, then wheeling and dealing will be right up your alley. Otherwise, practice to gain confidence every time you bargain. Notice that I said *every time you bargain.* At each sale you plan to buy something, you must bargain. It doesn't matter if it's 6 A.M. and you are the first customer. It doesn't matter if it's 6 P.M. and you are the last customer.

Always ask for a reduction. This chapter will discuss strategies for getting the lowest price that are proven to work even if you don't have previous bargaining experience.

TYPES OF PRICING

At the average sale, some items will have prices, and some items will not have any prices. At other sales, none of the items will have prices. How you bargain, with regard to pricing, will get you the better deals. At most sales, basically, nine types of pricing exist. They are

1. Priced as marked
2. Price, firm
3. Best offer
4. Best price
5. Sale price
6. Dealer price
7. No price
8. Make an offer
9. We're taking donations

I'll discuss the best way to get the lowest price for each type of pricing.

TIP: Always double-check a price that seems high. The item may be tagged incorrectly, especially if a lot of zeros are attached to the first number.

1. Priced as Marked

An organized seller will price most items. You certainly can negotiate the price. You may get a "No," but other than your feelings, it doesn't hurt to ask. On a piece that is marked with a price tag, always ask the seller the following question in one of the ways listed below:

- "Is that your best price?"
- "Can you do better on that?"
- "Is that price firm?"
- "Do you have room to negotiate?"

You really want the seller to make the first move and suggest a price because

1. The lower price that the seller suggests may be a great deal lower than what you would have offered. For example, if you see a brass candlestick holder that is marked $20, ask the seller, "Can you do better on that?" She may say, "$10," and you may have said, "$15."
2. If the lower price is not low enough, you can counteroffer. For example, for the same brass candlestick marked $20, ask the seller, "Can you do better on that?" She may say, "$15," you can counteroffer with, "$10," and the seller may counteroffer with, "$12."

2. Price, Firm

Firm price tags are attached to items when the seller

- Has paid too much for an item and doesn't have much room to negotiate
- Believes that the price is a true value and will take nothing less
- Doesn't want to bargain at all

A good example is the Boston rocker. You may run across a sticker that says $150 (firm) on a Boston rocker. This is a fair price for an original Boston rocker, made around 1840. However, many people believe that the Boston rockers that are painted black and stenciled along the back crest are old and valuable. Most of these black rockers were mass-produced, and are only worth about $60 to $80. Having knowledge in an area such as this will make you a better bargainer. You should also know that original Boston rockers are made of pine, show wear on the rockers and arms, have thicker pine seats, and the stencils of fruit or flowers are more crudely done.

You can negotiate on items that are marked "firm." Here are two ways to negotiate a firm price:

- a. Ask the question, "How firm are you?" Usually, the response varies, so be ready for
  - Someone who will not budge $5 on the price.
  - Someone who will say, "Come back after 2 P.M., and I'll lower my price."
  - Someone who will lower the price just because you asked.
- b. Show the seller that you're serious about buying a piece by showing him your cash and saying, "I'll give you $50 cash right now." Of course, most other people are going to pay cash too, but letting the seller see a $50 or $100 bill makes it hard to resist.

3. Best Offer

Best offer is used when the seller believes something is valuable or someone tells the seller before the sale that the item is valuable. In this case, the seller thinks

- *She can get big money for this item.* Perhaps, she saw a similar one on the "Antiques Roadshow" or her neighbor did, so the seller is convinced that the item is also priceless. Therefore, this method of best offer becomes, "Let's see what someone will give me for it since I really don't know what it's worth."
- *Something is wrong with the item.* If the piece, such as a motorcycle, has mechanical problems, and the buyer has to buy it "as is," a seller

will cover himself by taking best offers from several buyers and then notifying the individual who made the best offer.

- *The item is sentimental and worth a bundle.* Many people believe that because an item is old and has been kept in the family for generations, it is an antique and that antique means "valuable." This is not always the case, but you may have a hard time convincing the seller and may not be able to bargain with her at all.

Best offers usually are seen on automobiles, boats, motorcycles, and power lawn equipment. You may find some of these items at moving, estate, and multifamily yard sales. If you have time to research the item before making a best offer, then do so. Researching an item will let you know what the current value is in the market. Otherwise, a good rule of thumb is to go one increment higher than half the value the seller is asking (as long as you know that the item is not overpriced). For example, if an Old Town wooden canoe, painted green, is marked $500 or best offer, make an offer of $300. In rare cases, someone may make his best offer $501 because he knows that the canoe is worth it. Best offers that go above the asking price usually are seen in real estate transactions, not in personal property instances.

4. Best Price

Best price differs from best offer in the fact that you ask the seller for her best price, whereas in best offer the seller wants you to give your best price. For example, you see a purple carnival glass bowl signed N for Northwood at an antique show. The bowl is marked $225. You ask the seller, "What's your best price?" The seller may respond:

- "That is my best price."
- "Are you a dealer?"
- "I can take off $25."

As a buyer, you will have to decide if there is any money left in that bowl to buy and resell. A couple of strategies can be used to negotiate the price. If you show extreme interest in the piece, the seller may reduce the price because she wants the piece to go to "a nice home." You need to spend time with the seller and find out as much as you can about the piece. Ask such questions as, "Where did you get this piece? It's so unusual." Play dumb, as if you don't know anything about carnival glass. Many sellers don't like to sell to dealers because they know that the piece is just going to be resold. They would rather sell the piece at a lower price to "someone who will give their treasure a good home" than to someone in the business of making money off them.

Another strategy you can use is to ask the seller, "Do you have any other pieces that are less expensive?" And then compare the two pieces. The seller may negotiate her price on the first bowl and think, "Maybe, I had it priced too high anyway."

5. Sale Price

Antique sales or flea markets will have sale prices. Bright yellow tags with red lettering typically are used to indicate a sale price. Sometimes they are genuine sales, and 20 percent off the ticketed price is given, or it is a fake sale, and nothing has really been reduced, although you are led to believe that a sale is in progress. Often estate sales will reduce prices on the second or third day and call it a sale. Sometimes a sign is posted, "Sale—20 percent off," rather than marking each ticket. You can tell if the merchandise is brought in to "beef up" a yard or garage sale if you see these sale tickets with codes and numbers written on them. Then you may or may not want to dicker with an experienced dealer who wants to get rid of merchandise that is not moving in his shop.

6. Dealer Price

You might hear a buyer say, "What's your dealer price?" This refers to a discount for dealers who are in the business. Some co-op shops will give a dealer discount automatically (anywhere from 10 to 20 percent off the asking price), usually on items that are worth $10 or more. All shop policies vary, so it is best to ask the management. If you're not a dealer, you can still ask for a better price. The best way to do this is to just ask. Most co-op shops will call the seller on the phone if you make an offer below the dealer discount. Some shop policies are automatic, but sometimes you run into a dealer who is working her own booth. Then the seller may give you a discount to make the sale. Or if you ask nicely, you may get a discount anyway.

7. No Price

Have you attended a sale where nothing is priced and you wonder why? Sellers don't put prices on items because

- They don't have time to price items.
- They don't know the value of items.
- They make a value judgment based on your appearance in setting prices. (This is why you dress like you can't afford to buy anything.)

If you encounter this situation, you can do one of three things:

1. Ask the price of each item in which you're interested.
2. Gather all items in a box and ask for a group price.

3. Decide whether it will take too much time to find out the price and leave.

8. Make an Offer

Sometimes you will see a sticker that says, "Make an offer." What do you do?

    a) Do you offer what you think the item is worth?
    b) Do you make a low offer?
    c) Do you make a counteroffer?
    d) Do you let the seller set the price?

Most of the time the answer is (d). You want the seller to set the price. If you're unsure, say, "I don't know what it's worth." Try anything to make the seller come up with the price. If the seller doesn't give you a price, offer as low as you can. The seller may get insulted or reply with a higher price. Then you can counteroffer in the middle.

TIP: If other buyers or dealers are around, try to bargain without them overhearing your strategy. When a seller suggests a price that is too steep for your pockets, one of the best strategies to use is to make a snake-like hissing sound by breathing in through your teeth. In most cases, the seller almost always lowers his price.

9. We're Taking Donations

An organization that is raising money for a worthy cause often says, "We're taking donations. Whatever you can give will help." This is one of the hardest ways to bargain. You don't want to lowball the seller, but you also want to buy wisely. Therefore, you should approach this type of sale like any other. What is a fair price to pay for something and still make money? You can make sound buys and also feel good that you're helping someone in need. Whatever amount you decide on, don't let your emotions get the best of you.

THE AWARDS FOR BEST ACTOR AND BEST ACTRESS GO TO . . .

When it comes to bargaining, whether you're a seasoned pro or not, put on your acting cap and go for the Oscar. You may surprise yourself with your ability. I've included 10 role-playing strategies to get the best deal. Try different roles and see if one works better for you. Combine several of these roles, and adjust your technique to the item for sale, the seller's personality, and the situation you come across.

1. The Authoritarian

Walk in and act like you own the place. Don't be rude, but be firm. Let the seller know that you mean business. You're here to buy. You know what you want and how much you're going to pay for something. You breeze through the sale. You eye a fancy schoolhouse clock (see Figure 7-1) that says, "Old—$80." Politely, you say, "That clock is worth only $50 to me."

2. The Haggler

A pine drop-leaf table is marked $50. Quickly ask, "Is that the best you can do on that table? It's marked $50."

If it's early in the day, the seller may not budge or may say, "Make me an offer."

To which you respond, "How about $25?"

The seller counteroffers, "I have to get $40 for it."

Keep haggling and say, "How about $30?"

"You can have it for $35." The seller is a haggler too. You just have to respond quickly.

Figure 7-1 Schoolhouse clocks such as this one by W. L. Gilbert Clock Company, Winsted, Connecticut, hung in the one-room schoolhouses of the 1800s.

If you really want the item, you say, "Sold," and hand over the money.

If no other customers are around, and you think you can haggle a little more, say, "I'll think about it."

Sometimes, if the seller knows that you aren't going to buy the table, she may come down to your price and say, "Okay, $30."

You just knocked $20 off a $50 table that you know is worth $200. So why bother trying to get the piece at a reduced price? Most sellers expect to haggle with buyers. In addition, the seller may have marked the table up to $50, thinking it was only worth $20, so she really got $10 more than she expected. You never know what is in the mind of the seller until you ask.

TIP: Haggling makes you a savvy garage sale shopper. Haggle on every item you want to purchase. Remember to haggle quickly so that you can haggle again if you find another item or move on to the next sale.

3. The Complainer

Pointing out flaws in an item often will get you a reduced price. Use the complainer technique on any item that is damaged, stained, or torn. I don't recommend buying extremely damaged goods, but sometimes the "junkie" habit in you is so strong that you have to take that item home with you. Moreover, you may know of a way to fix an item that the seller doesn't know about. Figure 7-2 shows a man's 1950s jacket that cost only a few dollars because the jacket smelled of mothballs.

TIP: Be honest about the damage to or condition of a piece. Point out the flaws to the seller. You may get a few more dollars off the doll, quilt, or vintage dress because the item "smells old."

4. The Grouper

Often you can get a better price if you group items together. Try this technique when you buy more than one item or when the seller doesn't have much help and the checkout line is long. Instead of waiting while the seller adds up every little item, give him a ballpark figure. Of course, you've already added up the total, so round out your offer to 20 to 40 percent below the actual price. If this is too hard to figure out, go for half the marked price and see what happens. For example, you've found four or five different types of tools ranging from signed chisels to a plane. Each item was priced individually, with the

Figure 7-2   1950s jacket bought at a yard sale for $2 because the mothball smell was so strong that the owner wanted to get rid of it. The jacket is worth around $75.

total being $40. You quickly say, "Will you take $20, since I'm buying all of them?" Usually the seller will agree to your price. The seller won't take the time to add up each individual piece if he is swamped with customers. If the seller says, "Give me $25 for everything," you can respond, "If you throw in that set of screwdrivers." Always try to add in a little more to make the deal worth your while.

5. The Nibbler

Perhaps you feel funny or shy about making offers and bargaining with sellers. Try haggling once. Find one item you want, and try to get a reduced price on it. For example, if a scuba diving outfit is marked $20, ask the seller, "Will you take $10?" All the seller can do is say no. If you really want the outfit, ask the seller, "What's the best you can do?" The seller may say, "How about $15?" Then you say, "I don't know if it will fit me. How about $12?" The seller assumes that you want the scuba outfit for yourself. Don't tell the seller that you can barely swim and plan to sell the outfit on eBay. Or if it's a piece of furniture, you can say that you're not sure if it will match your decor.

TEA FOR TWO

Babs Connolly collects teacups and saucers. She likes the top end of the fine china made by Shelley, an English maker whose work dates from the 1880s. (See Figure 7-3.) Babs' husband, Danny, said, "When we hit the shows, we knew who was the better seller of Shelley. I didn't beat the seller down with the price. Everything was in great condition. She never put the hammer to us. Whatever she asked, I paid. I wasn't going to fight over a $10 bill."

6. The Questioner

You will learn to bargain better by asking questions. Questions unearth the family history about a piece or allow the seller to open up and talk to you. Ask the seller

- "Is this piece old?"
- "Where did you get this item?"
- "Was it in your family for a long time?"
- "What does it do?"
- "How does it work?"
- "Is that really the price on that item?"

7. The Agreer

At some garage sales, the seller will become the authority, and the best way to handle this situation is to simply agree with her. In this case, no matter what you say to the seller, she knows more about the merchandise she is selling than anyone else. Usually this is not true, but if you dispute her, you won't get very far. Make negotiating simple, and just agree with her.

8. The Distracter

I don't recommend this type of role-playing, although I know that it happens. The distracter is mentioned here in case you hold your own yard sale or set up at a flea market or show. A solo buyer, a couple, or a team will distract the seller to

Figure 7-3 Some Shelley teacups and saucers are worth up to $300. If you can't spot Shelley by pattern or shape, turn the cup over and look for the "Shelley" mark.

- Shoplift something
- Switch tags to get a lower price
- Buy something else cheaper

Keep your eyes and ears open. Pretend to tidy up your booth or space, and keep one eye on your merchandise.

9. The Disarmer

First-time sellers are just as apprehensive about selling as you are about buying. If you arrive earlier than the advertised start time, the seller may already have a defensive attitude. Go in with a cheery disposition, make small talk, and let the seller respond. He either will let you in, will tell you to come back in an hour, or will get out the shotgun (only kidding). Many sellers will go to extreme lengths to rope off their driveway and hang up their "No Early Birds" signs.

Another good way to disarm a seller is to take a child with you. The seller assumes that you don't know much or that you're shopping for kids' clothing and toys instead of any older items. Adults find it very hard to say "No" to a child if he wants to buy something. I usually make a joke about it and say, "My son is the early bird, not me." *Caution:* Don't bring the kids if you have mapped out 30 or more sales to hit on a Saturday morning. They will get too cranky, hungry, and bored, especially if they are little. When they are nine or ten years old and show an interest in collecting something, then they could go with you to a flea market to expand their education.

TIP: Dress your kids in old clothes too. If you look like you don't have any money to buy things, you may get a bargain just for that reason.

10. The Storyteller

Are you good at jokes? Can you remember stories from your father, grandfather, or great aunt regarding an old crock or kitchen gadget you see at someone's garage sale? Make a point of telling the seller so. The seller probably will take a stroll down memory lane with you. She opens up and feels good about selling a piece of her family heritage to someone who will take care of it or appreciate its history. You don't need to tell her that you're going to feature the item at your next antique show.

BODY LANGUAGE AS A BARGAINING TOOL

Another important aspect of wheeling and dealing has to do with body language, voice inflections, and facial expressions. Make note of the seller's body

AN "A-PEELING" AROMA

My father Bob Glass is notorious for relating old family stories. He was at a yard sale where a woman was selling what appeared to be a long-handled iron shovel. My father ran up to her and asked, "Madame, do you know what this is?" She said, "I have no idea." My father said, "My grandmother used one of these to remove hot oatmeal bread from the beehive oven next to the fireplace in her keeping room. The smell of the bread drifted out the window and down to the town, where the townspeople would line up every Saturday to buy her wonderful bread. How much do you want for it?" The woman chuckled and said, "For that story, Sir, you may have it for $5." My father walked away with a $95 item known as a *peel*. The funny thing is that story about his grandmother is completely true. See Figure 7-4 for an example of an iron peel used in colonial cooking.

Figure 7-4 A long-handled iron peel was used to remove bread from a beehive oven.

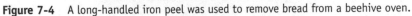

language because it will give you a clue as to how well you can bargain with him. This section covers the common body language you'll see at many different sales.

Sizing Up a Character

At a sale you will have to deal with different personalities. Whether items are priced or not, if both husband and wife are selling at the sale, you may find bargaining easier with the man than with the woman, or vice versa. At a multifamily sale, go to the older people first. Generally, their prices are lower, unless they are personally attached to a family heirloom—then the price may seem exuberant. Also, young couples may have little or no experience in selling. Strike a bargain with them, especially if they're selling items from a past generation. Whomever you deal with, body language will give you a clue as to your bargaining power.

Arms Folded and Crossed

A seller who sits by the cash box with her arms folded is not interested in talking to you. Find a way to get her to open up and relax. Bring over an item that you can't figure out how it works. Get her to unfold her arms, and then you can talk to her and ask for a reduction on an item.

Sitting with Legs Open

You can bargain all day with this type. They want to move their stuff. Strike up a conversation with them. They will bond with you and sell you something that came from their family.

Sitting with Legs Crossed

This seller is anxious. Be polite, and try to get him to stand up and reach for something you can't reach. Ask him a question, and point to a vase on the table and ask, "How much is that?" He will have to come over and examine the item. The seller's fears and anxiety will be diminished as he speaks to you. Your bargaining smarts are available now.

Scratching the Chin

If you make an offer on something and the seller responds by scratching her chin, you know that she is thinking about your offer and probably will say yes. Don't ask for a further reduction.

Raised Eyebrows

The seller is wondering why you made such a low offer on something. Give the seller an explanation as to why you offered so low. You might say, "I already have one, or I'm buying this book for my mother and I don't want to pay too much."

Incessant Talking

This seller is nervous about customers and sales. Chat with the seller if you can get a word in, but don't carry on a long conversation when he tells you about Aunt Betty who fed the birds every morning and starts to name all 100 of them.

Frowning

A seller who is already unhappy or grouchy before a sale starts is going to drive a hard bargain. Try to make small talk, and say, "I love this piece," or "Where did you get this?" Comment on the weather and say, "It's a nice day for a sale." Get her to smile or talk. If she feels comfortable with you, she may be more likely to negotiate.

Laughing

Sometimes a seller may laugh nervously or sometimes laugh boisterously to relax the situation. Laughing makes everyone relax, so if you find a piece or a

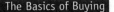

price amusing, laugh about it. You may have a good conversation that leads to a better deal because you and the seller laughed together.

Darting Eyes

Again, this is a sign that the seller is uncomfortable. He may not like dealing with the public or is unsure about prices. Try to ease the seller's mind by talking about how great everything looks. Focus on a particular item you want to buy. The seller may be more apt to look at the item than to look at you. You may find this a perfect opportunity to bargain quickly.

Now that you've turned a sale upside down and a seller inside out, what about the competition that shows no mercy and devours you and the seller in one gulp? How do you handle the competition and come out ahead? Read on.

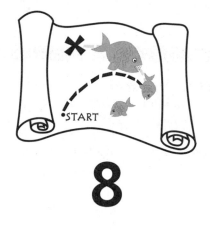

8

Swimming with the Piranhas

Piranhas are fierce fish that live in the Amazon River of South America. They have razor sharp teeth and swim in packs. They feed on weak and injured prey. Piranhas show no mercy and can devour an adult cow in a matter of minutes. In a feeding frenzy, some piranhas will take a bite out of their own kind. Sadly, some dealers who buy alongside you are like that. Yet you can swim with this ferocious species and, yes, even stay one split second ahead of them. If you're cautious, they won't bother you; in fact, they will barely notice you.

The comparison of a dealer to a piranha may be exaggerated, but on an infinitesimal level, some truth exists to this analogy. I've observed ruthless dealers who are rude to sellers and buyers, devour anything of value, and then move onto their next victim. You can learn to swim fearlessly beside these dealers or beat them at their own game—and this chapter teaches you how.

STAYING ALIVE

The best way to "stay alive," or ahead of the competition, is to increase your chances of finding the best deal. I've listed a few hints in previous chapters, including being an early bird (Chapter 1), plotting your treasure map (Chapter 3), and finding the bargains fast (Chapter 6). Here are a few more tips to keep you from drowning.

Go Undercover

A good ploy is to go incognito to the sales in your area. This is especially true if you live in a smaller community where you frequently see the same shoppers every week competing for items. I often wear a hat with a fake ponytail, dark sunglasses, and neutral clothing. In other words, don't draw attention to yourself. You can slip in and out of sales unrecognized by the same people you see every weekend. You can buy valuable goods and disappear before the dealers realize that you were their competition. For the same reason, drive a different vehicle and switch from a car to a van to a truck if you have more than one automobile in your household. Always keep the competition off guard.

Throw Caution to the Wind

When following yard sale signs, watch for signs that have been taken down or arrows that have been turned and are pointing in the wrong direction (yes, unfortunately, by other dealers). However, on the other hand, innocently enough, some signs have blown down in the wind, or the directions have smeared by the early morning dew.

To Park or Not to Park

When parking or not parking at a garage sale, heed these words of advice:

- On arrival at a sale, find the best parking spot. Sometimes you can park right in front of the driveway, even though the driveway is loaded with merchandise. The owner doesn't plan to go in and out of the driveway that day.
- Park your car so that you are heading in the right direction for your next sale. Or if you have a partner, have your partner drop you off at the sale while he turns around and parks the car.
- Park in front of the yard sale sign that is near the street. Most of the time this sign is at car level. You can block the sign from other dealers' view, and they may drive right by the sale, giving you a split second head start while they park farther away or turn around.
- Park out of the seller's sight, especially if you must drive your Lexus or Mercedes. Why? The price on that bedroom set just doubled because you look like you can afford to pay more for it.
- If you don't have your map with you, follow on the heels of another garage sale fanatic. Time your tailgating so that you can park closer to the sale sight, get out of your car first, and beat the competition to the sale. Here's where good knees and power walking come in handy.
- If five or six cars are already at the first sale in the neighborhood, park at the last house in the neighborhood sale and work your way in the opposite direction. You may find treasures at the end of the street because everyone else stopped at the first sale.

TIP: Drive a manageable car or truck. Some people will try to go garage sailing in their 30-foot RV. This takes extra time to back in and out of driveways and turn around while someone else in a small car has come and gone from a sale. In addition, it's a struggle to cram large purchases in your RV.

The Feeding Frenzy

Crowded sales are overwhelming for beginners. Don't be afraid to elbow your way in and look in the same box that someone else is hovering over. You may get a dirty look, but you have just as much right to look inside the box as anyone else—unless the person says, "I'm buying everything." Then shrug your shoulders and move onto another box. It's not worth getting into a fistfight, although, on occasion, tempers will flare.

To ease your mind and your chances of getting bitten in a feeding frenzy at a crowded sale, follow these simple techniques:

NOT A PRETTY PITCHER

A friend of mine named Jan who is a very respectable and fair dealer in the business went to a sale where two dealers both had hold of a Roseville pitcher. Neither one would let go until one of them realized that the piece was damaged. Then they both left the pitcher on the table after bickering over it for five minutes.

Roseville was produced in Ohio in the late 1890s until the mid-1950s. Most pieces are marked "Roseville, U.S.A." on the bottom, although earlier pieces are unmarked. Raised flowers and fruit are seen in later examples. The flowers found on these pieces include apple blossoms, bleeding hearts, dogwood, peonies, pinecones, snowberries, wisteria, and others. Roseville comes with blue, green, rose, and yellow backgrounds. Shapes include baskets, jardinieres, vases, candlestick holders, pitchers, and more (see Figure 8-1). At garage sales, you often can buy these pieces for $5 and under because sellers don't know their value. At auctions, you will have to pay a little more for Roseville pieces because more collectors will attend the auction when Roseville is advertised.

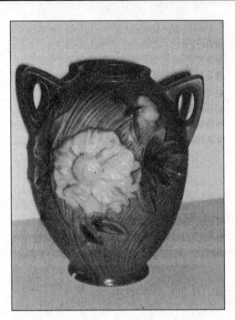

Figure 8-1 Roseville pottery is often decorated with raised flowers. Examples in excellent condition command good prices on eBay or at auction.

Stick It to 'Em
Have sticky labels in your pocket ready to attach to the furniture that you want to purchase. The label should say either "Sold" or "Sold to [your name]." Get big sticky labels so that someone else won't have sticky fingers and tear off the labels on pieces you have claimed.

TIP: If you've gathered a group of items and can't hold all of them, designate an area for your purchases in the corner of the garage or on the lawn. Throw your coat or blanket over the items to keep others from claiming what's yours. Alert the seller to what you're doing.

Go Fishing
Talk to the seller or, as we say in the business, "Go fishing." If the seller is unloading his merchandise from the vehicle, ask him, "What else do you have?" If he says, "Sports equipment." Ask him, "What kinds of sports equipment?" If he replies, "Toys, games, and basketballs." Ask him, "Do you have any big boy toys such as hunting or fishing equipment?" If he says, "No, nothing like that." You can deduce that it's probably not worth your time to

stick around while he unloads. Often, however, having a conversation will clue you in as to whether you should wait. Remember, you don't want to have a long, meaningless conversation with the seller. Extracting useful information, though, is beneficial to your buying ability and your "time is of the essence" strategy.

TIP: At flea markets and shows, the competition is intense. If you can get in early, try to "fish" at 5:00 A.M. while the seller is first unloading her van. By 8:00 A.M., the fishing is over, and the biggest "trout" are already caught.

Shop Around the Clock
Scan the tables and display areas both under and above the tables. I usually scan from left to right in a clockwise fashion. Are other buyers nearby? Scan the tables and displays that aren't drawing any attention. Are books your thing? Scan under the tables and in the boxes. Bend down and look. A lot of items are at 6 o'clock, right under your feet. And don't forget to scan at 12 o'clock, meaning on the walls of the antique booth or garage and above your head. I've purchased pictures, mirrors, horse tackle, old advertising signs, and tools because other people didn't look *above* eye level.

Keep Your Eyes Open
Learn by observing the prices on items. If something is priced unusually high and you don't buy it, make a note to look up that item in a reference book when you get home, or if you have time, ask the seller, "Why is that item so high?" You may get the family history or provenance on a blanket chest or discover something new about kitchen collectibles.

WHAT'S A MECKI?

It's certainly not a stiff drink, although, at times, you may need one. Annie, another friend of mine in the business, told me about a Mecki (see Figure 8-2). This is a tiny character figure with almost a porcupinelike face that is made in Austria. Most of them are labeled, "Original Peter-Figuren." A Mecki is only about 3 inches high and often is encased in a plastic dome. Many of them are in pairs. You can find these collectibles for a few dollars at garage sales or auctions.

Figure 8-2 A Mecki bride and groom doll set looks worthless to the average shopper but is valued around $150.

Cross the Line

If you're standing in line to pay for one item and have the exact change, see if you can pass others in line with armfuls of merchandise. Please do this with tact. You may upset other buyers or the seller if you appear impatient or uppity. Trust your instincts. If it's not appropriate to cut in line, wait your turn. This is especially true of church bazaars and rummage sales; the cashiers often are volunteers, the buyers are townspeople and/or church members, and a spirit of goodwill exists at the event. Don't be the only one who hasn't got the spirit.

TIP: At a rummage or estate sale, buy some old pillowcases for sale. Fill these cases with clothes and other intended purchases. Buy extra pillowcases and keep them stashed in your van.

Definitely "Not For Sale!"

Have you stopped at a sale, only to find that items are marked with signs that say "Not For Sale"? Do you just pass them by and not give them a second glance? Not anymore. Always ask about those items. When you go to an

I GOT IT FOR A SONG

I went to a sale where the owners had roped off a section that said, "Not For Sale." In the back corner was a musical instrument case in poor condition. It was partly hidden under some boxes of clothing. I asked the lady, "Is that case for sale?" She said, "Oh, no. I forgot all about it. My son said he didn't want that sax anymore and that I could sell it at the garage sale." I paid the woman $100 for the sax. I sold the instrument for $600 on eBay.

estate sale (one run by the family), sometimes family members don't have time to remove the items they want or have inherited, so they just put a "Not For Sale" sign on them. Once in a while, an entire room is marked, "Do Not Enter." Ask if those items are for sale. Family members may change their mind once they see cash coming in for other items.

See No Evil

A dealer may give you the "evil eye" because you're a new player in his territory and he feels threatened. The best solution is to ignore such people. They may talk about you for a while, but if you just go about your business, you'll get accepted as part of the competition. Then, on the other hand, some dealers, if they realize you are new in the business, may share their knowledge and give you leads on other sales and so on. This happened to me when I was waiting to get into a sale. Tom, a book dealer, said to me, "There's another unadvertised sale down the road that has the kind of stuff you buy." I said, "Thanks, I owe you one." I went to the sale and ended up buying several kitchen items, including a "pie bird" for a few dollars (see Figure 8-3). A pie bird is a small pottery figure, usually in the shape of a bird or a duck, positioned on the top of a pie to let steam out when the pie is baked. Prices range from $35 to $100 each.

More often than not you will come across the same dealers week after week. You will do better in the long run to be cordial to them. And remember this old saying, "One good turn deserves another." Pass on a lead to another dealer. There are enough slices in the pie for everyone.

Act As If You're Part of the Staff

Here's one of the best secrets I know to get you on the inside edge of buying opportunities. At garage and other sales, especially ones that are hosted by organizations, act as if you're part of the staff. In other words, casually start

Figure 8-3 Years ago, a pie bird was inserted into the piecrust and baked in the oven to let steam escape from the pie. Now collectors display pie birds on their kitchen shelves.

looking through the boxes of merchandise. Unwrap and display items on the tables. If you see something you want, carefully put that item to the side or back in the box you're distributing. *Caution:* You have to do this with tact; you don't want to get in anyone's way. Most organizations are short-staffed and appreciate the help. You could even ask someone in charge, "Want some help?"

TARNISHED OR NOT?

I stopped at a church sale almost an hour before the start time. Other people were milling around, so I followed suit, and within a few minutes, I had a box full of merchandise. One of the members asked me, "Do you work here?" I said, "No." She said, "You can't buy anything yet. The presale is only open to workers." Another woman said, "She's been here 20 minutes. Let her buy what she has in her box." Among other things, I purchased a Mexican sterling silver gravy boat for $2 and sold the piece for $175 at a sterling silver auction.

TIP: Volunteer at a community or church sale, where you may have the opportunity to tactfully buy things before the public.

The Bottom Feeders

Some professionally run sales will not reduce prices until the last day of a sale. Usually by the end of a three-day sale you can buy items for next to nothing. Don't go with the attitude that everything of value is already gone. Remember that you're not just buying anything old; you are buying anything that you can resell and make a profit on, even if it is to resell at your own garage sale. Often things are found at the end of a sale, and the owners will just let them go for a small amount of money or have a "free" box of items. Look to purchase old drapes, interesting light fixtures, collectible canning jars, shelves of flowerpots, or stacks of cordwood in the corner of the garage.

If You Can't Beat 'Em, Join 'Em

One way to get ahead of the competition is to become a "picker." A picker buys contents of barns, basements, and attics for a reasonable amount, turns around and sells his load to dealers, and makes a decent profit. The dealer then pieces out the items and sells them to the public for even higher prices.

Picking is a lucrative business if you're bold enough to knock on people's doors. You can go through a town randomly, knocking on doors, or call a seller if his number is listed in a newspaper ad. Pickers search out the seller's house a week in advance before his sale and try to buy. A picker is a good way

---

A DOOR-TO-DOOR TREASURES
AND TRASH COLLECTOR

Ronnie is one of the best pickers I know in Connecticut. He fills his truck every week by knocking on people's doors and asking them if they have anything for sale or anything they want to get rid of. He is kind of a door-to-door garbage man/salesman. He takes the good, the bad, and the ugly. Ronnie will sell at auction all the stuff he has picked in the last month. He gets good prices and always makes a decent profit. He will sell to other dealers, but he's learned over the years that he can make more money reselling the junk he finds himself.

"WE TOOK IT ALL!"

A husband and wife team in the business purchased only "leftovers" in a house. Instead of just buying the best, they told the owners that they would take everything, including mattresses, clothing, food, bars of soap, and the like. Their best deal was when they paid $500 for the remaining contents of an older three-bedroom cape. They found jewelry pinned behind the drapes, money in the mattresses, and old diaries from World War I stuffed in a shoebox on a closet shelf. They kept the brand-new refrigerator for themselves, and over the course of several months, they sold the rest of the "junk" for $5,000.

to become experienced because then you can become a dealer yourself instead of being the middle person.

FISH FOOD

Many dealers in the business are just like you and me—they have to eat! If some of them seem pushy, remember that they are just trying to make a living. Throw them a little fish food if you get the chance—tell them about a sale they might have missed or a place where you think they would do well selling their types of antiques. They may appreciate your honesty and become your friend and ally. And who knows what will come out of the favors you exchange. Don't you know that piranhas also make good pets?

9

Getting from the Garage into the Attic

So you've attended estate sales, auctions, or flea markets for some time now, but are you making the profit you envisioned? Buying a few pieces of glass and china at a garage sale and a few pieces of furniture at an auction will not necessarily fill your antique shop or keep you sustained as a "PowerSeller" on eBay for very long. As you have more money to invest, it's important to think of expanding your buying potential from not only the garage to the attic (and the cellar) but also to the entire contents of the house. A few secrets to open up doors to you, other than garage doors, are the focus of this chapter.

THE KEY RING

The opportunity to buy more than what is displayed or advertised at a sale may arise sooner than you think. What if you have the chance to buy the contents of the attic, the cellar, or the entire house? Don't say, "No, I can't do that" or think, "I'm inexperienced." This chance or good fortune could happen within the first month or the first time you go to a sale. Call in reinforcements, but when opportunity knocks and the door opens, walk through.

The Key to the Attic

To unlock the door to attic treasures, here are a few questions to ask the seller privately when you're at a sale:

- "Do you have any old magazines for sale, such as *National Geographic, Popular Mechanics, Ladies' Home Journal,* or *Saturday Evening Post*?"
- "Do you have any old trunks or suitcases?"

- "Do you have any cradles, beds, or bed parts you want to sell?"
- "Do you have any clothing, quilts, or blankets you don't want?"
- "Do you have any old typewriters or sewing machines?"
- "Do you have any encyclopedias or books that I could buy?"

Most of the items just mentioned are from generations of long ago, or at least you hope that is what the owners will show you. Some of the magazines I refer to are from the 1920s and 1930s and were never thrown out but saved, bundled, and stored in the attic. Some of these items you may want to buy, but generally, these questions are a way to get into the attic to see if any hidden treasures exist.

TIP: Call items "old stuff" instead of antiques. The seller will presume that you don't know much, and now is *not* the time to impress the seller with your knowledge; otherwise, he'll expect you to pay more.

The Key to the Cellar

If your community is in a geographic location in which the houses generally don't have attics but they do have basements, ask the seller if she has any

- Canning jars
- Old bottles
- An old wringer washing machine
- Flower pots or jugs
- Cast iron cookware
- Shop Tools

If you're lucky enough to get into the cellar, you may find old stoneware crocks and jugs, fishing equipment, musical instruments, and paintings, as well as stored furniture, including stacking bookcases, tables, chairs, and china closets.

The Key to the Front Door

In order to get the homeowner to let you in the attic or basement, it's best to ask a general question rather than a specific question, such as

- "Do you have anything else for sale?"
- "Are you bringing more items out?"
- "Is there something you can't haul out?"

BEAUTY IS IN THE EYE OF A FRIEND

Bob Glass, Jr., a well-known New England auctioneer, found an oil painting in the basement of a Southbridge, Massachusetts home. The painting and a few other items were labeled "for the dump" and placed behind the furnace. Bob immediately rescued the painting from the trash. The painting was a portrait of a man in golf attire who was the president of American Optical Company, located in Southbridge. On further research, Bob learned that the president's friend painted the portrait. The friend's name was Norman Rockwell. The painting sold for $33,600 and set a new auction record.

Often these questions will unlock the key to the house for you. Why? Because if the seller says, "Oh yes, I have a pine dry sink upstairs in my child's room that I couldn't bring down." You immediately say, "Can I see it?" And off you go, even though you don't buy furniture or have ever heard of a dry sink (see Figure 9-1). Why? You're going to get a house tour.

Figure 9-1 An old dry sink used in bathrooms before sinks were installed is now a decorative piece of furniture.

Try to get the tour alone and not with five other people who want to see the dry sink. This scenario actually happened to me, and I toured the lady's kitchen, dining room, and upstairs bedroom. I didn't buy the dry sink, but I did buy three lovely sterling silver dishes, a set of red ruby glasses, and English china that she wasn't going to sell until the following weekend. A dry sink is usually used in a kitchen or bedroom with a bowl and pitcher set displayed on it. The original dry sinks were used in colonial days before houses had running water. Another reason you want to examine the dry sink is because if there is an old bowl and pitcher set with four to six matching accessories in the dry sink, that could be a valuable bonus. Unfortunately, the dry sink was brand new pine, void of accessories, and carried a price tag of $200. But chances are the sink could have been an old one in original blue or red paint with a Johnson Brothers bowl and pitcher set. Maybe, next time.

TIP: If you live in a geographic area where the houses do not have attics or cellars, ask to see any furniture or anything that isn't moved easily out to the garage, such as pianos, stoves, or anything large and awkward that will get you into the house.

OTHER WAYS TO "BREAK INTO" A HOUSE

Of course, I don't mean this literally, but set a goal of trying to get into one house per month. This gives you four weekends to develop your buying initiative depending on how often you go treasure hunting. Like the role-playing techniques, for some of you, getting into the house will be easy. For others, who are timid, expand your paradigm. Either way, ask a simple question, such as, "Do you have any old lighting fixtures or canning jars?" The answer may lead you up a gloomy staircase through overgrown cobwebs into the dusty corners of the eaves or down the sunken stairway to the musty, dimly lit dungeon of the root cellar. Here's where the thrill-seekers or the "junkies" get high as they search for buried treasures.

BE SAFE, NOT SORRY

A few comments need to be inserted here regarding personal safety. Sometimes, if you are making a house call, a friend or partner can accompany you. This is a sound principle, especially if you're a woman. There is safety in numbers. However, if you have to go alone, consider taking a few precautions:

1. Trust your instincts. From your conversation or prior meeting with this person, you should have a general feeling or "gut instinct" about him.

2. Try to schedule the appointment during the day when other activity is going on in the area, that is, postal or UPS deliveries, school bus hours, and so on.

3. Ask the client a few questions prior to your meeting:
   - "Is anyone else going to be present to help load or inventory the merchandise?" (This will let you know if you will be one on one with the client or if a spouse or neighbor will be present. Get clarification on a first name so that you know if a male or a female will be present.)
   - "Is phone service available, or should I bring my cell phone if I need to make a call?" (This will alert you to the fact that the place has power and alert the seller that you have a phone.)

4. On arrival, have your cell phone ring or your pager beep from a family member or neighbor so that the client knows that someone else knows your whereabouts. Or make a call within the first minute of your arrival to verify your destination and location. Make sure that if the client's spouse is supposed to be in attendance, he or she is present.

5. If you still feel unsafe about going on calls on your own, carry mace or learn self-defense techniques.

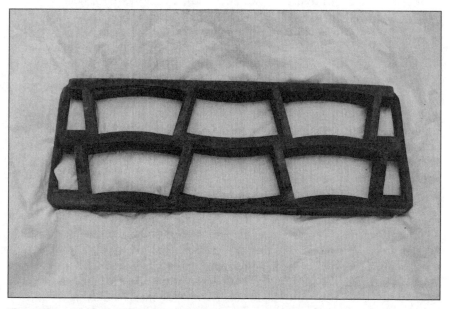

Figure 9-2 By getting invited into the house, I found this early wooden brick mold valued at $225 that to an untrained eye appears worthless.

BREAK OUT OF THE MOLD

By chance, I happened onto a yard sale on a back road. At 10 o'clock, the owners were still lugging things out of the house. I searched the tables and found an old phonograph.

I asked a woman who appeared to be the owner, "Do you have any records for this phonograph?"

She said, "I might have some in the basement. Are you interested in them?"

I said, "Yes." I really wanted to see what other trinkets were tucked away in the basement. What a jackpot! Not only did the lady have old records, but she also had furniture, pottery, china, glass, and a bonanza of other merchandise. She and her husband had hauled out items since 6:00 A.M. and were exhausted. Among other things, I bought a rosewood clarinet, red ruby glassware, an old yellow ware mixing bowl, some costume jewelry, and a wooden brick mold (see Figure 9-2).

You have to be willing to break out of the mold to find a good deal. Widen your parameters beyond what is only visible to your eye.

No matter what, always be aware of your circumstances. I have to say that in the 25 years that I've been in business, I've never had a problem or a situation that put me in danger because I trusted my instincts and was aware of the people and the environment of each house call. If I felt unsure, I would either bring a friend or cancel the appointment. Take necessary precautions, not unnecessary chances.

Lend a Helping Hand

At another yard sale I helped an elderly lady carry out boxes of merchandise because her help never showed up. I then unpacked the boxes and displayed those items on the table. I looked like I was part of the family. When someone asked, "How much for this?" I'd say, "Ask the boss," and I pointed to the lady. Every time I went back into the house, I put a few things I liked in a separate box so that I could buy these from the lady before I left. My hard work paid off: I helped a neighbor, and I made a week's pay in a day.

An Open Invitation

Win the trust of the sellers, and you win an open invitation to their home. Sellers appreciate courtesy and respect. They've worked hard to put their sale together. And you can show your respect if you

- Pay fair prices
- Act politely
- Strike up a genuine conversation

Show Them the Money

Place a small classified ad in the paper stating, "I will pay you $20 to look in your attic or cellar." Give your name and phone number. That's it. Your phone could ring off the hook. The idea is to get into the house because you most likely have to walk through other rooms to get to the attic or the cellar. But it's a good bet; you may find a collection of old Civil War documents or bisque dolls. So bring plenty of extra cash. If you don't buy anything, you must be true to your word and pay the person $20 for just looking.

DON'T LET IT GO TO YOUR HEAD

One Sunday morning I stopped at a garage sale because I saw some brightly colored material for sale at the edge of the road. I never bought the material but instead purchased over $1,000 worth of antiques and collectibles from the family. We got along so well that I now have an ongoing business relationship with them. The family invites me into their home every few months, and I purchase items from them to resell in consignment shops and on eBay. One of the best single purchases I made was a head vase of Jackie Kennedy Onassis that I bought for $30 and sold on eBay for $350. The family didn't know how much it was worth, and neither did I. I just liked the piece and felt that it was worth the $30 investment. I found out later that head vases or planters were used in florist shops as early as the 1940s. The heads were mostly of young woman with colorful hats (see Figure 9-3). The top of the "head" or hat was open to hold the flowers. Most of the vases came from Japan. If you are lucky enough to find a Marilyn Monroe head vase, it is worth $2,000 to $3,000.

Figure 9-3 Head vases from the 1950s and 1960s are a fun resalable item.

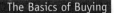 **TIP:** "Search through the classified ads and the 'Bargain Bin' section of the paper to look for washers and/or dryers for sale," says Steve Gass, a garage sale guru and treasure hunter from Connecticut. "Personally, I don't need any appliances; I just want to get into the house to see what else the owners will sell me."

A Special Word of Advice

Another way to get into a house is to ask for a certain item. In other words, ask about the specific area in which you specialize. For example, if a seller is still setting up and you don't see anything in your area of expertise, ask her if she has any of those items. A buyer once asked a seller if she had any cookbooks. The seller replied, "Yes, I have a bookcase full of them. And some of them are old. I'll show you." So the woman was invited into the house, had first dibs on the books, and a chance to buy other items. The rest of the buyers were speechless.

HE BOUGHT THE FARM

Every potential sale you stop at could have a key to unlock other doors of the house. Remember to ask questions, such as, "Is there anything you can't haul out that you want to get rid of?" Thus, when you think of a garage sale, think of the bigger picture—think about some questions to get yourself into the attic. Keep your ears open at each sale you attend. You may overhear someone say, "I have to clean out Uncle Joe's tools soon." And a friend might respond, "I have to do the same with my great aunt's books." That is your cue to jump in and offer your services. You may gain access to an attic in another house that hasn't been touched yet. Maybe Uncle Bill's garage sale is just a precursor to Aunt Mildred's basement, Grandma's attic, and ultimately, Grandpa's farm.

10

Specializing Wins Grand Prize

Are you overwhelmed by the amount of merchandise you could buy and resell? And you don't know where to begin? A simple solution is to specialize in one category that appeals to you. The more knowledge you acquire in that one area, the better your chances are of finding that item before anyone else does because you know what to look for. And you may pay more because you know what that item is worth and you're not just guessing or taking a chance. Eventually, with this knowledge, you will be earmarked as the expert. This chapter gives you resources and suggestions on how and what to specialize in to make the most money to boost the profit margin in your favor. To specialize, you need to become an expert. To become an expert, you need knowledge. To acquire knowledge, you have to read, listen, observe, and participate. And then to know if you acquired that knowledge, you have to make a few scores and, sadly enough, get burned a few times too. As one friend of mine in the business said, "If you're not making bad buys, you're not making good buys!" You may or may not have lost money on deals, but you will always remember

- The one that got away
- The one that someone else purchased
- The one you priced too low
- The one you made a killing on

When I traveled to London and visited several major auction galleries, I was amazed at how many young people worked in various specialized departments. During one tour, I asked a young man who was probably not more than 25 years old, "What makes you an expert?" He replied, "Because I say I'm one." Was he really an expert? Did anyone ask for his credentials, such as where he went to college, what organizations he belonged to, who he apprenticed under, or how long he'd been at his position? No! And would it matter? People believed him because he said so. He certainly acted as if he knew everything about early English silver, his area of expertise.

Maybe it's different in England, but to become an expert, I believe, takes a few years of being in the trenches, and still you miss some big ones. Even the experts can't know it all.

A JACK OF ALL TRADES

A great many people in the business are general dealers. They buy and sell everything including the kitchen sink. Walk into most antique shops, and the variety of items for sale is astounding. And you think, "How can they know so much?" The answer is they don't. Antique shops are another good buying opportunity once you gain knowledge beyond someone else's expertise. You may want to start with a specialization such as carpenter tools, but after some time, you may discover that all sorts of merchandise from furniture to linen to glassware are much more interesting and lucrative. It's an individual preference; just remember that someone else who wants to buy something from your general shop may have more knowledge in a particular field than you do.

TIP: When a new auction company or antique business advertises its grand opening, plan to attend. Your experienced knowledge and buying ability may shine as you cash in on some good deals from beginners in the field.

A STITCH IN TIME

Neil, another acquaintance of mine, went into an antique shop that had been in business for years. He bought a sampler (early stitch work usually done and signed by young girls) that was priced at $300 from a woman who supposedly knew antiques. Neil sold the sampler at a well-advertised auction for $1,200. Because he was an expert on needlework, Neil knew more about alphabetical and numerical New England samplers than the woman who owned the shop. Figure 10-1 shows an example of an early sampler. Rare samplers from the 1700s will command upwards of $50,000.

Figure 10-1   Keep a lookout for early samplers like the one pictured here.

INCREASING PROFIT MARGINS

Gleaning a general knowledge of antiques, collectibles, furniture, glassware, china, rugs, linens, toys, and other categories may pay bigger dividends in the long run, or it may not. Every situation is different. I know people in the business who have scored big as general dealers and others who buy and sell only early phonographs. If you're a beginner, however, focus on a particular field that interests you. You are less apt to make mistakes when you focus on one particular subject rather than on a broad range of antiques or collectibles. Learn about one category that interests you, such as vintage cameras, and then later expand into darkroom equipment, old photographs, daguerreotypes, and related books.

What Should I Specialize In?

The answer is easy and the result of a clear consensus among dealers and collectors. Buy and sell whatever

- You are passionate about
- No one else is buying
- You have knowledge in
- You can live with if you can't sell it

Here are some examples:

- Is music your passion? Buy and sell musical instruments, record albums, or radios.
- Are you interested in a particular sport? Buy and sell baseball cards.
- Do you have a hobby such as fishing? Buy and sell fishing equipment.
- Do other countries excite you? Buy and sell Chinese export items or Japanese prints.
- Do you love clothes? Pick a decade (1920s or 1950s), and buy and sell those styles.
- Are you a carpenter? Buy and sell old planes, chisels, and other tools.
- Do you work in a jewelry store? Take that knowledge and dabble in vintage jewelry.
- Did you study American history? Buy and sell Civil War military items.
- Were you an art major? Buy and resell twentieth-century oil paintings.

Narrow the Field

For every broad category in which you buy and sell, a collector's club or book is available on the subject. You can find these clubs online or listed in price books. I have given you a few in the Resources section at the end of this book. I encourage you to join a club because you can learn so much about one particular specialty. You could select furniture and then choose a certain era such as Victorian, a certain wood such as tiger maple, a certain maker such as Limbert, a state such as Pennsylvania, or a style such as twentieth-century modernism (see Figure 10-2). You can be broad or very selective within a category. For instance, you could focus on holiday items or, within that category, just Halloween items. If you are interested in Native American art, choose a tribe such as Plains, Sioux, or Apache and a category such as baskets, clothing, or jewelry.

Become An Apprentice

Believe it or not, you may have a gut feeling about some time period that attracts you. Follow that instinct. Follow your passion. Then become educated in the area that interests you. It's almost like going back to school. Read and study. Go online and do research. Take a course offered by a community college on antiques. Museums in your area may offer courses or have exhibitions you can study. Ask questions. And then get some good hands-on experience. In a manner of speaking, do an internship.

Become an apprentice, if possible. For example, if you want to acquire a general knowledge in antiques and collectibles, work in a group shop or volunteer as an auction assistant. Some states require that you apprentice

Figure 10-2   One of a pair of Danish modern chairs purchased at a garage sale for $20 sold at an estate auction in Connecticut for $3,000 or $6,000 for the pair. *(Photo courtesy of Robert Glass Auctions.)*

under an auctioneer before you can be licensed yourself. Go to auctions, go to flea markets, and go to shows. Observe what people are buying and what people are selling. Look at prices. Learn about items so that you can single out those treasures at yard sales or buy intelligently at shows and pawnshops.

Find a Mentor

If you're really a novice in the antique or auction world, ask a dealer or a collector if you can shadow him to see what he's buying, and soak up any information he gives you. Sean Seal, a young rug dealer from Connecticut, says that if you are interested in Oriental rugs, go to the countries where the rugs are made and talk to the weavers. Sean recommends reading books on the subject, but he also believes in hands-on experience. He says, "Examine the rugs, learn the patterns, touch the fibers, follow a dealer around, and be a sponge."

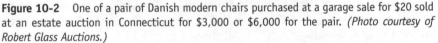 **TIP:** Barbara O'Connell, an exclusive dealer in jewelry, art, and early Connecticut memorabilia, suggests that you buy price guides in your area of interest and read them as you would a recipe in a cookbook.

SPECIALTY NICHES

Here are several hot areas on which to concentrate to make your profits soar. Please note that thousands of categories exist, and again, choose one that interests you or one in which you already have knowledge (that way you have a head start).

- *Aluminum.* Cheap to buy; the market hasn't taken off yet, many people are betting that it will.
- *Bronzes.* Statues, lamps, vases, anything signed, pieces from the Ming Dynasty and earlier.
- *Desk accessories.* Especially signed pens and gold pencils such as Waterman, Montblanc, or Parker.
- *Furniture.* Modern, retro, the 1950s; just peaking now but lots of good buys out there.
- *Musical instruments.* Learn the makers' student and pro lines; the difference is thousands of dollars.
- *North American Indian art.* Single tribes or regional areas, including baskets, clothing, and accessories, are untapped reservoirs.
- *Oriental rugs.* Big-ticket items to purchase, but there's a big payoff if you can gain respect from the rug dealers who control the market.
- *Paintings.* Signed oils, watercolors, modern, primitive; if you have an eye for it, the beholder could spend thousands that will go in your pocket.
- *Zsolnay pottery.* Glazed ware from Hungary, similar to colors by Tiffany; early pieces are rare and command hundreds of dollars.

TIP: Are you having a difficult time narrowing in on a specialized area? Toby Castle of "The One Man Band" recommends that you choose a category in which no one has written a book and become an expert in that field.

SPECIALIZED EXAMPLES

Below I've highlighted several examples of specialty areas. Choose your area of specialization, and apply the following techniques to your specialty niche to make the most profit.

The Crown Jewels

If you had some of the crown jewels, you wouldn't need to read this book. However, here are several tips to keep you searching for that diamond in the rough. A few tools that will help you buy wisely are

- A loop or magnifying glass
- A diamond tester
- A gold tester
- A digital jewelry scale

I recommend carrying these items in your car (except in extreme heat or cold). If you go to an auction with jewelry and silver, you most likely can use your digital jewelry scale (ask permission first). Many auction houses will state whether an item has been tested for gold or if it is a diamond. Tools of the trade, such as a diamond or gold tester are available for purchase at a jewelry supply store, by mail order, or on the Internet. Check the Resources section at the end of this book for further information.

When you go to a sale, ask the seller

- *"Do you have any junk jewelry?"* Why? Most sellers don't know if they have valuable jewelry. Many sellers refer to their jewelry as junk that has been stashed away for years in a drawer. Good jewelry gets mixed up with the junk jewelry. And the great, signed costume jewelry pieces are also mixed in. In addition, if you say "junk jewelry" and the sellers have any knowledge, they will tell you exactly what they have.
- *"Do you have any fine jewelry?"* Often sellers won't bring out the really good jewelry because they know that a yard sale is not the place to sell it. Often they will have the good pieces tucked away in a safe in the house or in a safety deposit box at the bank. If you have the credentials, offer your services.

Ginger Castle is a graduate gemologist (G.G.) who recommends that you take several courses offered by the Gemological Institute of America. The main office is in California, with a branch in New York. Home study and

EXTRACTING GEMS AT ESTATE SALES

At professional estate sales, as at any sale, good buys exist. The professionals won't know everything, especially if you chose to specialize in a particular field such as paintings, Oriental rugs, duck decoys, or jewelry. I went to a professional estate sale and bought a blue brooch for $32 (see Figure 10-3). Miriam Haskell, a twentieth-century costume jewelry maker from New York, signed the piece on the back. The pin is worth $200.

Figure 10-3   Miriam Haskell and other signed costume jewelry pieces are very collectible.

on-campus courses are available on pearls, diamonds, colored stones, or a combination if you want to get your G.G. designation. The certification is recognized worldwide as the standard in the industry. See the Resources section in the back of this book for contact information.

Tool Time

Buying an old tool to sell is different from buying a tool to use. If you can capitalize on the fact that collectors will pay more for tools than a dealer trying to sell the tools to the public, you can make money. Dan Connolly, a master carpenter from Shrewsbury, Massachusetts, and collector of old tools, says, "I bought only the best. I didn't collect old tools until I was 65, but I collected the top end. The first tool I bought was a Stanley, and I paid $1,250 for it."

To buy tools, remember that collectors look for

- The quality of the tool
- The age of the tool
- The patina of the wood
- The condition
- Certain makers
- Early signed tools

TIP: Knowing the size and shape of a Stanley number 1 plane if you saw it at a garage sale could pay your mortgage for one month. Figure 10-4 shows you the size of a Stanley number 1 plane.

The Real Thing

Of course, along with specializing or any type of buying, be aware of reproductions. A reproduction is something that is new but made to look old. Reproductions hurt the value of older, unique, original, and one-of-a-kind pieces because they are no longer the only one on the planet.

Reproductions exist in many categories. A few examples include

- Coca-Cola items
- Coffee grinders
- Mechanical banks
- Milk glass items
- Flow blue china
- Currier & Ives prints
- Decoys
- Roseville pottery

Figure 10-4   A Stanley number 1 plane is worth about $1,800.

John Glass buys and sells Coca-Cola items. He has learned through hands-on experience the difference between real Coke items and reproductions, especially when it comes to trays. John says that the main thing to look for is the placement of the trademark. In the early trays, the trademark symbol is within the C in Coca. Reproductions place the trademark below the C. Figure 10-5 shows an original Coke tray. Figure 10-6 shows a reproduction of the same tray. Please note that the original advertisement on the 1926 tray says, "Drink Coca-Cola," whereas on the reproduction the advertisement says, "Delicious and Refreshing."

The Lure of the Fisherman

A great deal of interest has surfaced in recent years in fishing equipment. Good pickings exist at local flea markets, yard sales, and auctions. Try specializing in saltwater or freshwater fishing, fly-fishing, or a combination. Specialty fishing books have surfaced recently to aide you in your search for that hidden treasure.

Figure 10-5 This original 1926 Coca-Cola tray is worth about $1,000.

Figure 10-6   1973 reproduction of the same Coca-Cola tray is worth about $50. It's important to know how to tell the real thing from the knock-off. *(Photos courtesy of John Glass.)*

To the ordinary eye, a number of flies look like they wouldn't even catch a fish, but fly tying is a specialized art, and many collectors seek out flies tied by certain makers. Carrie Gertrude Stevens, a housewife from the Rangeley Lakes Region of northwestern Maine, first tied flies in 1924. For 30 years she tied flies, invented 24 streamer patterns, and created a unique fly that became known worldwide as the Gray Ghost Streamer. Her flies, if you are lucky enough to find the originals, are tied at the head with jungle cock (a bird from China) and are not glued down. At the start of the eye, the fly is tied in black, red, and black (see Figure 10-7), making her flies distinct from those of other tiers.

TIP: When targeting your specialty area at flea markets or shows, you may find that those items (such as flies or fishing lures) are mixed in with general merchandise. Chances are that the seller is not as informed about those pieces, and therefore, the prices may be reasonable. Usually, you will get a better buy at a general vendor who has fishing equipment than at a vendor who is selling only fishing equipment.

Antique Aluminum?

Aluminum items fall short of being antiques and are not sought after as eagerly by collectors. Such items also fail to fit into the Arts and Crafts Period, where prominent makers of items of copper and other metals lead the way. Many people are banking on the idea that aluminum items will reach a

Figure 10-7   Two hand-tied flies by Carrie Stevens of Rangeley, Maine, are worth $500 each.

recognized and important status in the metal industry and thus in history. But who's to say?

Early aluminum items date to the 1920s. The hand-hammered or hand-forged pieces signed by the makers are more collectible (see Figure 10-8). Designs include pinecones, bamboo, flowers, and figures such as horses, dogs, and ducks. Many of the pieces were stamped and numbered by the manufacturer. Some of the better-known names and companies are Arthur Armour, Buenilum, Continental, Bruce Cox, Everlast, Farberware, Wendell August Forge, Kensington, Rodney Kent, and Palmer Smith. An aluminum associa-

A TRUE GARAGE SALE "JUNKIE"

Every year, Jeff attends one of several antique shows at the Minnesota State Fairgrounds to search for aluminum pieces. He met a woman who was also an aluminum collector. When Jeff revealed to her that he had over 1,000 pieces, she remarked that her garage was filled to capacity with 7,000 pieces.

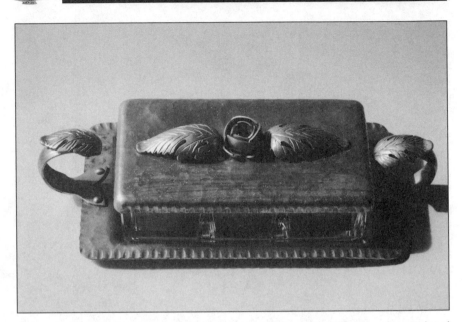

Figure 10-8   Fancy hand-wrought aluminum-covered dish with divided glass insert, signed and numbered by Continental.

tion, a newsletter, and several reference books are available. Consult the Resources section in the back of this book.

Jeff Glass, who has collected aluminum for 15 years, recommends buying

- A designer you like, in case you have to keep it for a while
- Pieces that are complete, that is, complete lazy Susan sets with covers
- Unusual or rare pieces, such as tables, mirrors, and waste baskets
- Items that are in good condition and not badly scratched or dented

Jeff says that the best place to find aluminum is at flea markets, garage sales, yard sales, and thrift stores. You can still purchase hand-hammered aluminum pieces between 99 cents and $5, with most pieces valued for resale at $25 to $100.

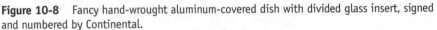 **TIP:** Check for senior discount days in thrift stores and Salvation Army stores to get up to 25 percent off items.

TIP: Keep in mind when you buy an item where you are going to sell that item, so you don't become a compulsive collector instead.

A SPECIAL WORD OF CAUTION

Another downside to specializing is that you don't want to specialize in an area that may not amount to anything, although at the time it is all the rage. An example is Beanie Babies. Sure, they have collector tags, come in cases, and have price guides, but they are barely holding their value. However, 100 years from now, they might be the next collectible trend.

You could specialize in a few different areas. Perhaps you have an interest in stoneware crocks and jugs, cast iron cookware, and Fabergé eggs. Hone in on all three specialty areas so that your eggs aren't all in one basket, so to speak.

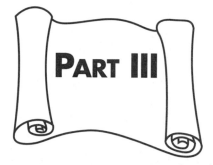

PART III

MAKING YOUR BIG PROFIT

*(Photo courtesy of Treasures Antiques & Collectables,
106 Rt. 122, Amherst, Hew Hampshire
Rick and Sherry Tobin, owners.)*

11

Understanding Trends and Establishing Value

What if you don't have a clue what an item is worth? How do you find out? A number of resources are available to you. Don't rely on just one method. For example, check eBay "sold" prices and also check current price guides. A close range of value between the two sources may give you a solid idea on what to ask for your item. A further range of value would suggest that you should visit a few antique shops or consult an expert. This process is time-consuming but recommended to establish value and obtain top dollar. You don't want to have seller's remorse and find out later that the large Oriental urn you bought at a yard sale for a few dollars and sold for a few hundred is actually from the Ming Dynasty and worth $200,000.

FINDING OUT WHAT IT'S WORTH

Here are a several ways to find out what your treasure is worth:

- Search the Internet.
- Check eBay for current and sold prices.
- Use price guide books or current and past auction catalogs.
- Go to the library or bookstore to find reference material on the subject.
- Visit shops, shows, or flea markets for similar items.
- Consult an expert in the field.
- Request an auction estimate.
- Get an appraisal.

Internet Search

Welcome to the world's most extensive research library. Almost any subject you want to research can be found on the net. You can do a search using a search engine such as Google, Yahoo, or Dogpile.com. Go to the net, and where it says "Search," type in an item you want to research. For example, perhaps you bought a painting signed by John Hilton. Go to Google, and type in "John Hilton." You will then be given the results of your search, in this case 1 to 15 of 400,759 results. Glance down the listings and find one or two sites that list an artist, in this case the second entry, "John Hilton—Artist Painting Prices, Art Appraisal, Artist Paintings [AskART.com]." Then click on AskART.com. The information that appears shows a sample of his artwork and his birth and death dates. Of course, to find out any current prices, you have to subscribe to the service. Figure 11-1 shows a John Hilton painting that was purchased at an auction for $500 a few years ago and is currently worth $5,000.

eBay Search

Another way to research items is to do a search on eBay. You actually can find out how much someone spent on a specific item on eBay by looking at the final sale price of an auction. eBay's prices are only kept on the Web for 30 days. Go to the Web and type in www.ebay.com. You can type in either a completed listing for prices realized or click on current items to see what is up for bid this week.

Figure 11-1 Western artist John Hilton's landscape entitled "Smoke Trees" is valued at $5,000. *(Photo courtesy of Robert Glass Auctions.)*

1. First click on "Search" in the header.
2. Click on "Completed listings only."
3. Click on "Price: highest first."
4. Next sign in to eBay as a new user or type in your user ID and password if you are already a member.
5. The page will list small photos, known as "gallery photos," with a brief description of the item, pattern, age, and so on.
6. Click on a specific picture or line, and you will automatically go to that page for more detailed information.

For example, a search on eBay for Clarice Cliff resulted in 1,413 items found that week with final sold prices. Clarice Cliff was an English pottery maker in the art deco period whose patterns of bright colors and geometric shapes were unlike anyone else's. Since many pieces are sold from Great Britain, a conversion chart is already in place on eBay so that you can see the U.S. dollar amount. Clarice Cliff items (808) were up for bid. If you want to see how many Clarice Cliff jugs are offered in the bizarre ware pattern, type in "Clarice Cliff Bizarre Jug," and 13 jugs pop up (see Figure 11-2). The more specific information you have, the better results you will obtain.

TIP: If you have a similar item on eBay, wait until that item sells because the price could jump several hundred dollars or more in the last five seconds of the bidding. In that case, click on "Watch this item in my eBay," which will automatically post the selling price when the auction closes.

Price Guides/Reference Books/Auction Catalogs

You have to start somewhere to evaluate prices, and reference books in your particular field of interest will give you a baseline, as well as a brief history on a particular manufacturing company or crafter. You'll find a list of several price guides in the Resources section at the end of this book. *Beware:* The prices cited in these guides are not necessarily a selling price; they are just a starting point on evaluating value. Many individual prices in these books give a range of value. For example, according to Judith Miller's *Collectibles Price Guide 2004,* a 1929 World Series game ticket and program issued for game 1 in Chicago has a value range of $1,500 to $2,000. Many price guides have great color photos and background information that are extremely helpful to beginners.

Current and/or past auction catalogs with prices realized are available from most auction galleries. Some auction results are free, and others are available for a fee. Some catalogs are available to download from the company's Web site. For example, single auction catalogs from Sotheby's range

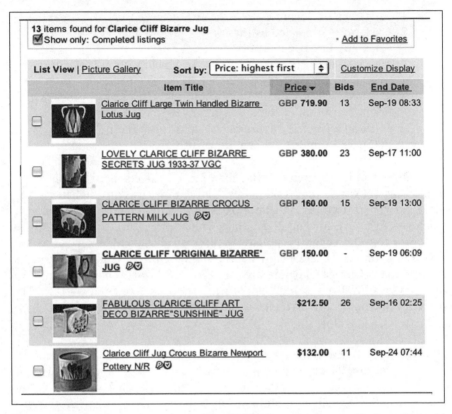

13 items found for **Clarice Cliff Bizarre Jug**
☑ Show only: Completed listings   • Add to Favorites

List View | Picture Gallery   Sort by: [Price: highest first ⬍]   Customize Display

	Item Title	Price ▼	Bids	End Date
☐	Clarice Cliff Large Twin Handled Bizarre Lotus Jug	GBP **719.90**	13	Sep-19 08:33
☐	LOVELY CLARICE CLIFF BIZARRE SECRETS JUG 1933-37 VGC	GBP **380.00**	23	Sep-17 11:00
☐	CLARICE CLIFF BIZARRE CROCUS PATTERN MILK JUG 🐾🗓	GBP **160.00**	15	Sep-19 13:00
☐	CLARICE CLIFF 'ORIGINAL BIZARRE' JUG 🐾🗓	GBP **150.00**	-	Sep-19 06:09
☐	FABULOUS CLARICE CLIFF ART DECO BIZARRE"SUNSHINE" JUG	**$212.50**	26	Sep-16 02:25
☐	Clarice Cliff Jug Crocus Bizarre Newport Pottery N/R 🐾🗓	**$132.00**	11	Sep-24 07:44

Figure 11-2 A completed search on eBay will give you prices on specific items that sold within the last 30 days.

from $12 to $50. If you wanted all of Sotheby's jewelry sales worldwide for the year, you would pay $614 with a discount of 15 percent. For a subscription to an auction company's catalogs, visit the auction company's Web site.

Go To the Library or Bookstore

The library is an excellent research center as well. Many large libraries are online, and you can find whatever subject you need to research. But many people prefer to go directly to a library and physically pick up a book and read about a particular American piece of furniture from the 1700s or a particular maker. For instance, when I researched some information about Wallace Nutting, an American furniture maker and photographer from the early 1900s, I came across his autobiography. I was so fascinated by his life

THAT'S JUST DUCKY!

Jim Hutchinson, an avid decoy collector from Connecticut, has over 60 reference books on decoys. Of all the different specialties he collects, Jim has profited the most with duck decoys and shore birds because he is well informed and self-educated about makers in a particular region, thanks in no small part to his extensive reference library.

story that I borrowed the book for two weeks. The same hands-on interaction is true of bookstores. Many dealers and collectors like to have a physical reference library at home or in their shop rather than a disposable one online.

Visit Shops, Shows, or Flea Markets for Similar Items

In general, go "antiquing" and observe what other dealers or collectors have priced their goods. Go to some of the high-end shows to get a feel for the market and what's selling. Don't just look at the items; read the price tags, ask questions if the item has a high price, and then do comparison pricing with eBay and price guides. If you're just doing research, resist the urge to buy something unless you know that "it's a good deal." Keep in mind that items that seem like they are one of a kind may not be unique. Clark van der Lyke, an eBay PowerSeller, resisted the urge to buy a Hollywood clapboard (used on old movie sets) when it was offered at an auction in Connecticut. He did a search on eBay and found 300 such boards that week up for bid in California. His "unique" East Coast item was commonplace on the West Coast.

Consult an Expert

Again, if someone is willing to be your mentor, you can learn a tremendous amount about a specialty field, and along with that learning comes an understanding of the prices and values of items that are rare and collectible. Ellen Rubell, who is known as "The Wedgwood Lady," is passionate about Wedgwood (fine English porcelain first made in 1759). Ellen said that when she first started, she thought that Wedgwood only came in blue but soon discovered that Wedgwood was made in every color of the rainbow. Lilac is her favorite. She belongs to several Wedgwood societies, started one of her own, and attends Wedgwood conventions to keep abreast of the market. People from across the United States, England, Australia, Canada, and

Japan consult and buy from her. Many people from around the world visit her home-based shop in Wallingford, Connecticut, to study and enjoy her extensive collection. She is now a mentor to others who are passionate about Wedgwood.

Request an Auction Estimate

Many auction companies, especially the larger houses such as Sotheby's and Christie's, will give auction estimates on your item if it were to be offered at their auction. The auction estimate is usually free, although some houses have limits on the number of items. Most houses require a photograph for evaluation. The main drawback is that you may have to wait up to six weeks for the estimate. If you live in New York, Los Angeles, or close to a major city, you can schedule an appointment and maybe see a specialist sooner. An auction estimate is only an opinion, and the opinion may change on physical inspection of the object.

Get an Appraisal

Another expert that can help you with regard to value is a certified appraiser. Many auction companies also have appraisers on staff. You can find these experts listed in the Yellow Pages or in a national directory. Many of them will belong to a society such as the International Society of Appraisers or the American Society of Appraisers or become a certified personal property appraiser with a designation such as Graduate Personal Property Appraiser or Graduate Gemologist.

Appraisals can be expensive because they are a legal document prepared for insurance, tax, or other purposes. Most appraisers work on an hourly or per-item rate (anywhere from $100 to $300 per hour). If you have an extensive collection, the appraiser will come to your home and give you a preliminary review as to the extent of the appraisal and fee. Appraisals consist of descriptions and per-item values with a summary page of value and the appraiser's credentials. Basically, two types of appraisals exist:

1. Fair market value
2. Insurance replacement cost

Fair Market Value Appraisal

This is an estimate based on what a willing buyer and willing seller would pay if neither one was under duress to buy or sell. The fair market value is often an auction value because that value is considered fair market. Many fair market value appraisals are done for estate tax purposes when a family member dies and the personal property needs an evaluation for taxes.

TAG THIS GRAPEFRUIT SWEET!

Ed attended a tag sale where a gentleman had a set of six Tiffany gold-washed grapefruit spoons for $65. A local jeweler had appraised the spoons at a fair market value of $130. "I'm selling them for half price," the man said. Ed, a dealer in American silver, paid him for the spoons and consigned them three months later to a Boston gallery, where they sold for $575. As a word of caution, appraisals are also just someone's opinion and as in this case, the appraiser missed the mark.

Insurance Replacement Cost Appraisal
This is an estimate based on the replacement value of an item for insurance purposes if that item were to be destroyed, damaged, or stolen. This appraisal is advised on items you're going to keep rather than sell on the open market.

A SMALL PRICE TO PAY

When it comes to pricing, everyone has his own system or methodology. First, let's examine the outside factors that affect price, and then we'll examine what I call the "inside factors," or what you paid for it versus what you can sell it for.

The Outside Factors

Many factors affect price, and the outside factors are the ones that you have little control over. Some of these factors will hurt the value of an item, such as reproductions. Some of these factors will help the value of an item, such as a hot trend. Here are a few specific outside factors that affect price:

- Economics
- Provenance
- Trends
- Reproductions
- Nonfunctional to functional
- The seasons

Let's examine these factors more carefully.

Economics
The economy definitely influences people's buying habits. People always have and always will buy and sell items. The quantity and quality of goods may

fluctuate, but really great antiques are a good investment if and when you need to sell those items.

TIP: Phil Liverant, a well-respected and eclectic dealer for over 50 years, recommends that you buy one good-quality piece a year, something that gives you visual pleasure, such as a good painting or a well-crafted piece of furniture. Phil believes that over the last 25 years, good antiques have outpaced any other form of investment. Phil says, "Collect what you like, but collect good. That's where you can make your money, no matter what the state of the economy."

Provenance

The more you learn about the provenance—the history of a particular item, such as what part of the country it came from or if it belonged to anyone famous or local—the more the item is worth. So anything the seller can tell you is helpful, and anything you can discover on your own could make several hundred or several thousand dollars difference. The price guides and the experts on "Antiques Roadshow" confirm that if you can attribute a piece to a certain maker, region, tribe, or so on with documentation, the piece is worth more.

TIP: To obtain the best price for an item, try to research its history. Visit museums to further your education and therefore your buying power.

Trends and Fads

If we could all predict the next trend or fad; we'd be rich too. Nevertheless, it is possible to notice rising trends. Often you can ride the wave of a trend because trends can last for several years or several decades, whereas fads tend to come and go more quickly, although the same fad could return in 30 years. Keep abreast of trends in the marketplace through

- Fashion
- Gift and catalog stores
- Magazines
- Retail furniture stores
- Cable and TV shows

Magazines such as *Martha Stewart Living, Country Living, House Beautiful, Country Home, Yankee*, and others show clever ways to make

DEATH ART IS NOT HANKY-PANKY!

Several years ago, Laurel M., an antique dealer who conducts business under the name "Through the Looking Glass," went to a moving sale in Washington, D.C. She bought a box containing several lace hankies, each priced at 25 cents. One had an embroidered scene of an old urn and had some names and dates written below it. Laurel had seen similar hankies displayed at the Rockefeller Museum in Williamsburg, Virginia. The hanky, known as *death art*, was done in the 1800s by a family member who embroidered a scene on a handkerchief and inscribed the birth and death dates of a deceased relative—a rather morbid but beautiful tribute. Laurel sold the hankie to a private collector at an antique show for $450.

antiques practical and decorative. Visiting stores such as Cracker Barrel (a chain of country restaurants with attached gift stores up and down the East Coast) also will alert you to trends and reproductions on the market. Contemporary retail stores such as Pottery Barn, Crate and Barrel, and Pier I Import also set trends, such as when white leather is in, dark pine is desirable, or painted white furniture is hot. Check out the latest styles in furniture and fashion because the retail stores carry the latest craze. For instance, you can purchase real Italian leather furniture at an estate sale or country auction for less than half of what it would cost you in a retail department store and take that set to your local consignment shop and triple or quadruple your money.

The morning talk shows also feature decorators, fashion experts, and antique dealers who discuss upcoming trends, often on a seasonal basis. Rhinestones were once considered "shabby chic," and that drove the prices up. Nowadays, you can buy rhinestone necklaces for $5 and $10. At present, gaudy pins are in and are used to accent scarves, jeans, and blouses. Retro is hot now, but by the time this book is published, retro may be out, and something else will have taken its place. *Retro* refers generally to the years from 1929 to 1968, with current emphasis being on the forties, fifties, and sixties. Watch these trends, and then go and buy these items. But don't wait too long to turn around and sell them. Trends tend to drive up the price because those items are in such demand and everybody wants to jump on the bandwagon. If you jump on the bandwagon first, you could have a very nice ride.

GREEN WITH ENVY

The once-collectible opaque green dishes known as Jadeite, made by Fire-King and marked on the base or with a paper label, were popular in the 1940s through the 1960s but are now being reproduced and sold in stores such as Cracker Barrel. The reproductions hurt the collectible market, and the resale value on old Jadeite pieces has dropped owing to the new manufacture of these items.

TIP: *Country Home* magazine publishes a top 10 list of what's hot in antiques and collectibles in its July–August issue every year. The magazine also lists emerging trends. Cash in on the trends, buy these items, and sell them to collectors. Don't wait too long, thinking that the price is going to get higher. Make your profit, and go on to the next trend.

Reproductions

Sadly enough, some people don't care if an antique is a reproduction. They just want something that looks like the "real thing" and aren't concerned with value or investment. And that's fine, but reproductions hurt the market. When anything new is produced, usually the value of something old plummets. Exceptions occur, but for the most part, the old and unique item is not so unique anymore.

Nonfunctional to Functional

Designers in New York and other cities scour flea markets to find unusual items to refurbish and sell to their clients at a profit. *Family Circle* magazine in its April 2004 issue found 15 items at a flea market and refurbished those items to make them functional and beautiful. One example was to strip down ugly and uncomfortable ornate chairs, paint them white, and cover them with red and white gingham. If you have this designer's eye, then you may be able to capitalize on designer decorating the old-fashioned way. Shows such as "Oprah" and "Extreme Makeover: Home Edition" often feature designers and innovative ways to decorate using old antiques. The secret here is not to decorate your own house, but to buy items others will like and sell those unique items to them.

For example, anything that relates to the kitchen is a sure bet on a trend, especially items used in a clever manner. Recently, sewing machines with the

THE LIGHTER SIDE OF IRONING

Priscilla Gimple, from White Lake, Michigan, buys old wooden ironing boards and paints full-size historical lighthouses on them (see Figure 11-3). She signs and numbers each board. Her lighthouses command over $200 at auction. Not bad for a $5 investment plus her time.

black cast iron treadle bases were a hot trend. Decorators purchased the sewing machines for their fancy scrolled base rather than for the outdated sewing machine. In most instances, the sewing machines were removed, and a marble slab was used as a top. The fancy new stands were sold as plant stands and bakery tables to knead bread. Another example is a pair of ice tongs, once used to add and remove chunks of ice from the icebox, now used as a paper towel holder in a country kitchen.

Figure 11-3 Useless antique ironing board turned into a showstopper. This ironing board is the Boston Lighthouse and is number four in Priscilla Gimple's series.

TIP: Observe what people use for decorations on their lawns. Old steamer trunks filled with flowers and old red- or green-stenciled wheelbarrows are hot accents in landscape design. Steamer trunks are easily purchased for $10 or less. Wheelbarrows are a little pricier, but ones in good condition you can resell for $150 or more.

The Seasons

The highest grossing month in retail is December, with January usually following a close second. If you realize that people may have more money during December and January, you may be more apt to sell items on eBay or in your shop during these times. "If you follow the retail trends, you could increase your own sales," says Helen Louth, owner of The Hope Chest in Johnston, Rhode Island.

The holiday market not only changes seasonally, but also within the holiday realm are certain collectibles that become hot. Remember the cabbage patch doll craze? You couldn't buy one at Christmas for under $500. Today they are sold at yard sales for a few dollars. A recent collectible trend is the Annalee dolls. These cute dolls with elflike features were made in Meredith, New Hampshire from the 1950s to present day. If you know the tags and rec-

Figure 11-4 An Annalee elf doll is worth $50.

ognize the features, you can find these for $5 and under. Figure 11-4 shows a 1970s Annalee elf that Donna bought for $1 at a church Bazaar. The doll is valued at $50. Ones that are signed by the maker, Barbara Annalee Thorndike, are worth much more.

TIP: Again, read the magazines and see what's hot for the holidays. Most holiday magazines come out months before the actual holiday. This will give you a good lead time to buy these items cheaply and market them to customers with the hefty profit going in your pocket.

The Inside Factors

Many factors affect price, and the inside factors are the ones that you have more control over. For example, if you research an item, you can control the price yourself. Or if you put a reserve on an item up for bid, you can control the minimum price you will accept. Here are a few specific inside factors that affect price.

- Research
- Double or nothing
- Reservations, please
- The high/low theory
- Pull a number out of a hat
- The fudge factor

Let's examine several of them more closely.

Research

When you research an item, you'll have a better idea of how much to price that item. You control how much time and research you put into a piece; thus you decide price, at least at flea markets, shows, or your own shop. On eBay and at auction, you can have control on the price to some degree if you sell the item with reserve. If you let the item go unreserved at auction, you take your chances. Don't cry when the fat lady sings, and it isn't your song she's singing.

Double or Nothing

Many people in the business use the *double rule* when it comes to pricing their merchandise, and this is based on what they paid for the item. They don't have time to look up their item in a book or consult an expert. They are perfectly happy if they can double their money. Hurrah for the next buyer who steps in and buys their items and makes an even higher profit because the first buyer was too lazy or ran out of time to research something valuable.

A BORED GAME!

Barbara Lee-Roberts, a dealer in the business for over 30 years, bought an old Monopoly game for $10 at a yard sale. She priced it at $100 and took it to a show. It didn't sell. She took the game to a toy convention and priced it at $300; it didn't sell. She then tried several other avenues (this was before eBay) and shopped the game around for two years. She set up at a local flea market and priced the game at $10. Another dealer came by and said he'd give her $5 for it. She accepted, and that was the end of the story, right?

Wrong. The dealer then took the board game to the "Antiques Roadshow," where the expert told him that he had an early game worth around $3,000. The man said that the lady he bought the game from didn't know anything. However, Barbara replied, "It's only worth what someone else is going to give! He probably still has that board game today."

Again, so you don't fall into this trap, research an item, get a second opinion, or search eBay for like items sold and the amount. If you're in a group shop, peruse other booths to see if any item is comparable with yours. Check prices before you offer your item for sale. In some cases the reverse occurs, and you'll find that your item will have to be priced less than double or it won't sell because the market won't bear it.

Reservations, Please
Some dealers are afraid they have paid too much for an item, and to prevent themselves from getting burned, they sell the item with a reserve. They set the minimum price they will accept. This happens at auctions (including eBay) where an item isn't sold unless it reaches a preset value. Sometimes the items never reach that value, and then what do you do with the item? Often you sit on it for a long time, or let it go for a lower price eventually. On eBay, you can relist your items and place a lower reserve or let the item go unreserved.

The High/Low Theory
This has to do with marketing an item rather than the concept of buy low and sell high, although that is a valid theory also. Of course, there are exceptions. One dealer named Don from Massachusetts said, "I buy cheap, but I also sell cheap. That's the only way I've been able to survive."

The high/low theory is when something is priced too low, people may not look at it. When an item is priced too high, the person may not nibble either. So do one of two things:

1. Either move the item to a new location, either within your booth or to another show, or
2. Change the price tag, either higher or lower than the price presently marked.

Again, this doesn't mean that you are guaranteed to get the price if you fluctuate one way or the other.

Pull a Number Out of a Hat

I knew a father and son team who used to pull numbers out a hat. One would say, "What should we mark this?" The other one would say, "I don't know," and they'd reach up into thin air and magically pull down the number from the sky. Their prices were literally out of the sky, but believe it or not, most of their magically priced items sold. Remember, you can always come down on something that is priced high; you just can never go up. I advise using this method only if you can't determine a price by any other means. This method is a risky guess rather than an educated guess.

TIP: Ed Correia, owner of Under the Pine Antiques and Collectibles shop, advises you to price things according to your purchase price. Ed says, "I can't mark up items and sell things for thousands of dollars. I have a conscience. I price antiques so that I can sell them and the customer is happy."

The Fudge Factor

I think we all dream of that "pie in the sky" item and certainly want to tell our friends, neighbors, and others in the business about our big success. So we might fudge the numbers a little bit and brag a little more about something that we purchased for very little and then sold for a lot of money. I see this trend on eBay. Most people I've talked to about eBay brag about how great it is and how much money they've made. I've only heard a couple of people say, "eBay is a pain. You have to answer all those picky e-mails. You end up in the packing and shipping business. Some weeks you make a good profit, and then the next week you don't make ten bucks." It's like going to the casino or the racetrack: Everybody brags about how much they won, never about how much they lost.

RELATIVELY SPEAKING!

When pricing has you stumped or in a quandary, don't be in a big rush to sell something. You now have several resources to use, including price guides, the Internet, libraries and bookstores, shops and shows, and other dealers or experts in the field. And when you weigh all the factors that affect price, including economics, trends, and your own gut feeling, you have a lot to consider. But so did Einstein, and when it comes to the big picture, it's all relative anyway.

12

Selling Your Treasures Through the Experts

The next two chapters focus specifically on locations to sell your merchandise. I've called this chapter "Selling Your Treasures Through the Experts," and in this approach you actually trust others to sell your valuables. These options include auctions, group or co-op shops, consignment shops, and estate sales. Chapter 13 talks about selling your treasures on your own and discusses all the places where you can sell things yourself, including eBay, flea markets, shows, garage sales, and single-shop ownership.

I've run the gamut from selling at flea markets, auctions, shows, co-ops, consignment shops, garage sales, and classified ads. Although I have my favorite places to sell, I don't limit myself to one particular venue, and neither should you. Most of the places I'll discuss are viable places where you can sell merchandise, providing you've done your homework. Research the items, the method, the location, and the management.

YOUR MERCHANDISE IS IN GOOD HANDS

To get to the nuts and bolts of selling, I have included the following selling options. The rest of the chapter details each method and the pros and cons of each way to reach your final customer.

1. *Auctions.* These are live, face-to-face auctions at a gallery or hall where the bidders determine the price unless you have a reserve on the item up for bid. (eBay is geared primarily toward do-it-yourselfers, although many companies have started their own upload businesses in which they will take care of everything regarding eBay;

you just have to bring them the merchandise and pay them a commission. eBay is discussed in Chapter 13.)

2. *Group or co-op shops.* In this situation, although you price the items yourself, in most cases you are not the person selling the items, unless you are required to spend so many days in the shop as part of your contract.

3. *Consignment shops.* The staff is responsible for the pricing and selling at consignment shops. Hopefully, upper management or someone who has some background in antiques, collectibles, and trends in the marketplace will price your items.

4. *Estate sales.* If you are just starting out, you will want to employ an estate sale specialist rather than trying to run one yourself, although you eventually could aim for this goal. (Another option for an entire estate is an auction.)

THE AUCTION METHOD

Going once, going twice, going three times . . . sold. This famous line, used by auctioneers, makes the auction process exciting not only for the buyer but also for you as a seller if you have items up for bid. Auctions have several different levels from fine art and antiques in the city, to the specialty auction held in a hotel ballroom, to the little on-site auction in the country.

Prestigious auction houses are centered in major cities around the world. The most well known ones are Christie's, Sotheby's, and Bonhams & Butterfields (formerly Butterfields & Butterfields). On a smaller scale, regional and local auction companies are also making their mark, providing quality sales and service.

Basically, to sell something at auction, you should first

- Become familiar with several auction houses and observe how they "run their ship."
- Send a photo to get a "thumbs up" or "thumbs down" on your most valued treasure. The auction house or company will give you a free presale estimate if it makes the cut as to the minimum accepted consignment value. Some of the minimum consignment values are in the low thousands.
- Obtain an appraisal if you're dealing with an estate situation or want a second opinion as to value.

Before You Sign on the Dotted Line

Before you consign anything and sign a contract, ask the auctioneer or company manager the following questions:

- *Do you have a Web site?* Most auctioneers will have a Web site to advertise their sales and send out e-mail notices to customers about upcoming auctions. Web sites maximize exposure of goods for sale to millions of users. Many auction companies have "live" online Internet bidding to reach even more potential customers.
- *Do you advertise nationally?* Some weekly and monthly antique publications are nationwide. The *Antiques and Arts Weekly*, more familiarly known in the trade as "The Bee," is located in Newtown, Connecticut, but has a national base and a reputation as being "The Bible" for auction sales. Regional newspapers, such as *Maine Antique Digest* and *Antique Trader Weekly* in Dubuque, Iowa, reach beyond their own states to bring buyers and sellers together.
- *Do you sell items with reserves?* Many auction companies will sell items to the highest bidder. If you have an item that you think is worth a great deal of money, find an auction company that will sell with reserve, meaning that if the item doesn't sell at your agreed-to price, it is returned to you. Of course, check to see if any charges accrue if the item doesn't reach the reserve price. *Caution:* You still have to find a market for the item if your intention is to sell it in the first place.
- *What's your commission?* Some auction houses charge as little as 5 percent. A few auction houses charge nothing because they make their commission on the other end from the buyer (the buyer's premium). But commission rates vary from company to company because there is no set percentage in the business. So expect to pay anywhere from 5 to 50 percent. That's a broad range, so you need to shop around not only for the best commission rate but also for an auctioneer who has an honest reputation.

TIP: A lower commission doesn't always mean that you will reap the most profit. Take heed of the saying, "You get what you pay for."

- *What other fees do I have to pay?* You don't need to worry about this as much with smaller houses, although they may charge insurance, storage, and moving fees. Don't be afraid to ask about the fees up front.
- *How soon will I get paid?* Some auction companies pay you within one hour after your items are sold (general consignment auctions), some pay at the end of the sale, and others will pay in 10 or 20 business days or take up to a month (35 days at the top galleries).

TIP: Always make sure that you have a copy of the contract and that the parties, you and the auctioneer (or an auctioneer's representative), have signed it. Also request an inventory list in exchange for the items the auctioneer now has in his or her possession. Don't let the auctioneer say, "I'll send you the list when I inventory everything," unless you are very comfortable with the auctioneer and have sold items previously through that firm.

Dealing with the Big Houses

So just how can someone work with the big auction houses? For starters, if you have access to the Web, you can visit most mid- to large-sized auction companies and read their policies, upcoming sales, and contact information. For instance, type in www.alderferauction.com. The home page that comes up will have a menu including sale categories, auctions, selling, publications, services, company background, and help (see Figure 12-1). Once you feel comfortable reading about a company, ask an auction goer or an antique dealer if they've dealt with the large auction houses and their experience with them. Then call or e-mail the company and find out its consignment and commission rates. Once you're satisfied, make an appointment if you live close by, or send or e-mail them a photograph of the item you want to consign.

Figure 12-1   Maneuvering around a Web site of a major auction house is easy. Just click on any subheading, and most of your questions will be answered.

The Pros of Selling at a Big Auction House
- Knowledgeable specialists have experience in the international market.
- Extensive advertising alerts dealers and collectors of upcoming sales.
- A higher dollar amount may be realized because of publicity, wider markets, and reputation.

The Cons of Selling at a Big Auction House
- If you have a great item, you may have to wait six months to a year until that specialty auction is held.
- Major galleries put reserves on items based on their knowledge and expertise. If the item doesn't sell because the reserve isn't met, it could take another four to six months before it is offered again at a lower reserve. And you may be charged unsold lot fees (sometimes 5 percent of the reserve price).
- Other charges are incurred, such as for illustrations, pictures for the online catalog, shipping, handling, insurance, and service charges (These costs add up, so find out these charges up front.)

What's Your Best Guesstimate?

Many of the large auction galleries will give free estimates on the type of property they sell. Each auction house has a minimum acceptance value within each specialty department. They request that you (1) attend an appraisal clinic, (2) make an appointment, (3) mail in a photograph and an auction estimate request form (available on their Web sites), or (4) e-mail a description and photograph. Some auction galleries limit the number of items. The turnaround time for an estimate is three to six weeks. The estimate is not to be used for legal purposes. For that, you need an appraisal. If the item is not seen physically, the estimate may be adjusted if the item is consigned to a future sale.

TIP: When you sell at auction, always ask for a "trade" commission. If you regularly conduct business with an auctioneer, he may reduce the commission rate for you.

Dealing with the Little Houses

First and foremost, visit a few of the auction houses and companies in your area. Find out which ones have a good reputation. Talk to people who have consigned with them or have attended their auctions for some time. Check with the Better Business Bureau to see if they have any complaints filed against them.

The Pros of Selling with the Little Guy
- You may get more personal attention.
- There may be a quicker time frame to sell your goods.
- Prices may be fairer.
- Settlement may be sooner (meaning a check or cash for your property).

The Cons of Selling with the Little Guy
- Some items could be misplaced, damaged, or broken.
- Advertising exposure may be local and limited.
- Your item may sell under its value owing to a lack of bidding participation.
- Expertise and experience may be lacking.

CO-OPS OR GROUP SHOPS

Another option besides auctions is group or co-op shops. In some parts of the country, these group shops are known as "antique malls." Selling out of a group shop is different from selling out of your own shop. Many people prefer to sell out of group shops for a variety of reasons. Listed below are the pros and cons.

The Pros of Selling in a Group Shop
- You don't have to "man" your booth or be present to sell items.
- You don't have to deal with the public or answer their questions.
- You don't collect any money.
- You don't have to worry about reporting state sales tax (some group shops take care of this).

SO VAIN!

Robert Glass, a well-known Connecticut auctioneer, had a client who wanted to sell an old six-owl weathervane from his barn. Bob sent photos to three prestigious auction galleries, who turned down the weathervane, believing the minimum consignment reserve of $5,000 would not be reached. With his client's okay, Bob sold the weathervane at his own antique auction. The weathervane sold for $27,500 and set a new record at the time. Moral of the story: If a major auction house doesn't have faith in your item and you do, search for someone who shares your opinion.

The Cons of Selling in a Group Shop

- You may not sell as much because you can't use your "super" sales pitch.
- You have to refresh your merchandise every couple of weeks.
- You may have to do "shop time" on the floor (check with the shop for rules).
- If someone makes an offer on a piece and the shop calls and you aren't available, you might lose a sale.
- The space is usually small.

So Little Space

If you want to try your hand in a group shop, start in a small space, maybe just a couple of shelves in a showcase. Once you are comfortable and make a profit, go to a hutch or floor space. For variety, you can sell out of several group shops in different cities or different states to see if another location is more profitable.

A space may be small, but with a little artistic flair and management of space, you can cram in a lot of merchandise without having it looked cluttered. In Figure 12-2, antique dealer John Dinsdale of Fox Hill Antiques has made great use of a small space.

Figure 12-2 This dealer has used the booth space to the maximum without having it look cluttered.

TIP: Gail Peterson, owner of Jeffrey's Antique Co-Op Mall in Lunenburg, Massachusetts, says, "The dealers who take pride in their booths with an array of quality fresh merchandise normally do better than those who do not work their booths as much. Display—Quality— Price—Make your booth interesting enough so people want to stop and look and not walk by."

Sizing Up the Price

Spaces in a group shop vary from the size of a showcase, to a hutch, to floor space, with the price climbing for each larger space you desire. Usually the rate is monthly. Some shops will prorate the monthly rate if you rent in the middle of the month. Some shops require a security deposit of one month's rent also. And then when you leave, you are asked to give a month's notice. But each shop is different, so ask the manager. Expect to pay $40 to $150 for a wall cabinet showcase depending on the number of shelves (some are locked, lighted, and alarmed), $75 to $125 for a hutch space, and $150 to $300 for floor space depending on how many walls you request. Many dealers rent more than one size space. Prime spaces, such as ones that have front window space, cost more and usually have a waiting list. In the larger cities, you will pay more for less space. Some group shops charge a rental and a commission fee, which you can offset if you do "floor time" in the shop. Other group shops will hire you under a separate contract if you want to work in the shop.

To Consign or Not to Consign

Before consigning to a group shop, observe and ask the following:

- *Is the owner accommodating and glad to welcome you to his establishment?* Do you get along with the manager? Is he cordial and helpful? Or is he too busy? Keep in mind that you could have a long-time relationship with this person, and you want the communication lines open and comfortable.
- *What are the security measures taken so that items don't get stolen?* Some shops
  - Require that you lock your purse and bags in a locker or leave them in your car.
  - Have video surveillance cameras.
  - Search any bags or boxes that dealers remove when they refresh their stock.
  - Employ all three security measures.

- *On any given day, is there a high volume of traffic outside the group shop as well as inside?* (See Figure 12-3.) Location and traffic flow inside and outside the shop are extremely important. Are weekends busy with no place to park? Are the aisles filled with people searching for bargains?
- *What is the ratio of dealer sales to retail sales?* If the shop has a high retail traffic flow, that means higher dollars for your sales because the dealer discount does not apply to retail buyers. Of course, you don't have to deduct any percentage off your items. Clearly mark on the tag "net" next to the price or in the space where you would write the dealer discount.
- *Is there a waiting list to get a space, or are many booths for rent?* A group shop that has 150 to 175 dealers may be filled to capacity, and you may be placed on a waiting list. This is a good sign. You know that dealers are happy and merchandise is selling. If a lot of spaces are for rent, then there may be a management or other problem, such as inadequate advertising or poor location.
- *May I talk to someone who rents space?* Make a point of speaking to someone who has rented a space in the shop for a while. Ask how that person likes selling in this shop, what he thinks of the manage-

Figure 12-3   Jeffrey's Antique Co-Op Mall is located on busy Route 13 in Lunenburg, Massachusetts, which contributes to its busy traffic flow both inside and outside the shop.

POSITIVE POSITIONING

Over the years, Peggy Russ has consigned to several different group shops and feels that location within the shop is very important. She likes to be in the front, near the checkout counter, for a couple of reasons: (1) The traffic flow is higher, and (2) the staff is more likely to keep an eye on her merchandise.

ment, and how business has been over the last four to six months. Gross sales vary from month to month owing in part to the economy, summer vacations, weather, and so on.

General Shop Policies

Policies vary from shop to shop, but in general

- Your rent is due on the first of the month.
- You are paid either once a month or twice a month.
- The shop will contact you with offers, which you may accept, decline, or counteroffer.
- Returns usually are allowed only if an item is not marked correctly.
- If credit cards are used, a 3 to 5 percent surcharge is assessed to you the seller.
- Sometimes locks are furnished for showcases (often a one-time fee applies, which is refundable when you leave).
- The shop assumes no responsibility for loss, theft, or damage.
- Booths should be serviced preferably twice monthly.
- Some shops request all booths to decorate with timely themes, that is, seasons or holidays.

TIP: Some shops are known as "juried" shops and request that you bring in photographs of your merchandise and have an interview with them before they let you sign up.

Guidelines for Tags on Merchandise

The tags that you attach to your merchandise must contain certain information in certain designated areas on the tag (see Figure 12-4). Guidelines for these tags vary from shop to shop, but in general

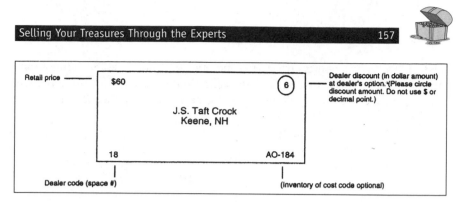

Figure 12-4 Guidelines for tags in a group shop are very specific, such as this example provided by Antiques at Colony Mill in Keene, New Hampshire.

- Merchandise must be ticketed in a standard format.
- Damaged merchandise must be noted on the tag.
- Reproductions also must be stated on the tag.
- Use a new tag if you change the price.
- Use removable stickers, not ones that adhere fiercely to the item.

How to Get More Sales in a Group Shop

Many factors determine whether someone will stop and look in your booth, but you can help customers decide by doing the following:

- Have an artistic and inviting display.
- Participate in the months that the shop intermittently holds "sales."
- Refresh your booth or change items around at least every other week.
- Have an unusual or curiosity item to draw customers into your booth.
- Educate your customers with descriptions and information about each item.

TIP: Marylynne D., who is a former landscape designer for Sheraton Corp. and is now a part-time floral designer and antique dealer, likes to give customers visual examples. In her booth, she adds a flower arrangement or plant to an old chamber pot or wicker basket to give customers suggestions on what to do with something old. Sometimes people want to buy the floral arrangement too. Marylynne is happy to accommodate them because those people will buy from her again.

CONSIGNMENT SHOPS

A variation on the group shop idea is the consignment shop, although you don't have a separate space and you don't pay rent. Instead, you pay a commission. Many consignment shops encompass a mixture of items from antiques to contemporary, including jewelry, china, glass, furniture, kitchen items, books, and clothing. Some shops specialize in one area such as

- Children's toys and apparel
- Big boy toys
- Home furnishings
- Furniture
- Clothing

TIP: Many consignment shops have brochures that list all the consignment shops in the state. Check at the counter for any relevant literature. Visit different shops and get a feel for the types of merchandise they sell, ask to look at a contract, and find out their commission fee.

The Pros of Selling in a Consignment Shop
- You don't have to set a price.
- You don't have to watch items.
- Consignments are accepted daily.
- You drop off the items to them rather than have people drop in on you.
- Items are intermixed with other items and displayed in a showroom-like setting.
- Your consignment is kept in the shop for three to four months for maximum exposure.

TIP: Donna Matteson has sold in consignment shops for five years. She says, "I don't have to price it. I don't have to watch it. All I have to watch is the expiration date, and then I pick up my check or I pick up my stuff."

The Cons of Selling in a Consignment Shop
- Often the staff is very choosy when it comes to accepting items.
- Consignment appointments book up quickly, and you may have to wait several weeks for an opening.
- Your item could be returned to you or donated to a charity at the end of the time frame.
- Often you have to deliver your own furniture and put it on the floor (sometimes the second floor).

- The commission deducted from each item sold is usually high—expect between 30 and 50 percent.
- Pricing is usually well below retail (to attract customers), and pricing is always lower than what you would price an item at a show or in an antique shop.

Items in Demand

I have talked mainly about antiques and collectibles, but used furniture and household items sell extremely well in consignment shops. So the next time you go on a buying spree, keep in mind the following items that are in high demand at consignment shops:

- Accessories (upscale bags, shoes, hats, and belts)
- Baby furniture and equipment
- Clothing—children's, career, maternity, name-brand and designer (under two years old), and vintage
- Costume and gold jewelry
- Drapes and fabric
- Furniture—living room, dining room, and bedroom sets
- Gift boxes, bags, and baskets
- Lighting and lamps
- Oriental rugs
- Porch and patio furnishings
- Toys and games
- Wall art and pictures

THE WOW FACTOR

Helen Louth, owner of The Hope Chest in Johnston, Rhode Island, says that when people come into her store, she wants them to go, "Wow." She follows the retail trends. If the retail stores play music, she plays music. If the color black is hot, she has plenty of items for her customers to choose from. If someone wants to consign something and asks, "How does it work?" She replies, "Quite well." Her store sells 2,000 to 3,000 items per month, so she is always looking for new consignors. The interior of her store is shown in Figure 12-5.

Figure 12-5   The Hope Chest in Johnston, Rhode Island, displays gently used furniture and accessories in a showroomlike atmosphere.

Ten Steps to Consignment Success

1. Call and make an appointment. Most shops are located in the Yellow Pages, or you can find them by going to the Web and typing in "consignment shops" and a state.
2. For furniture, first e-mail or bring in a photograph.
3. Convey how many items (or boxes of merchandise) you have so that you are allotted adequate time (some shops do not inventory on the spot, and you have to leave the items).
4. Clean all items, and get rid of any musty smells.
5. Make sure that all pictures have hooks or wire for hanging.
6. Make sure that nothing has sharp edges.
7. Do not bring in chipped or damaged items.
8. Be on time for your appointment so that the owner can keep to her schedule.
9. Be gracious about items the shop rejects (you can try again next week or even go to another consignment shop).
10. Have patience if a staff member is pulled off your job momentarily to attend to store business.

ESTATE SALES

Some communities frown on auctions, as do some clients. Some people don't want to lug things to a consignment shop. An estate or professionally run tag sale is a viable option for people who want some kind of protection on their merchandise, want a certain amount for the contents, or have to dispose of an entire estate because the relative has passed away. (A true estate sale is where someone in the family is deceased.) If you're new in the business, you can work out a business arrangement with the specialist who runs estate sales.

The Pros of Selling at an Estate Sale
- An expert sets the prices (so you're not at the mercy of fluctuating auction prices).
- The specialist has time to research items.
- The entire event is completed usually in one weekend.
- Any valuable leftover items can be sent to an auction in a neutral location.
- Leftover items can be bid on and removed by a "junk" person.

The Cons of Selling at an Estate Sale
- Many hours are spent on sorting, arranging, or pricing items (an hourly rate may become exorbitant).
- The dumpster charges on trash removal may outweigh the profit margin.
- A buying frenzy occurs in the first hour (the most likely time for stolen or unpaid-for goods).
- Extra help is needed to watch different rooms so that items don't "walk."
- Someone has to handle money, make change, and write out receipts.

Some estate sales are advertised on the Web. Companies send out e-mails as well as newsletters and brochures to preferred customers about their upcoming sales. Company profits are based on a flat fee or a percentage of the gross sales, anywhere from 10 to 30 percent depending on the time frame involved. Helen Louth, an estate sales specialist, conducts estate sales and either (1) will come in and price items based on an hourly rate and let you run the sale and collect the money or (2) for a commission will do it all from arranging, pricing, and day-of-sale selling.

To find someone who conducts an estate sale, look in your local news-paper, do a search on the Web, or look in the Yellow Pages. Some auction companies and antique dealers will run estate sales. Helen Louth has a sign in her consignment store that directs people to ask her about having an estate sale. Otherwise, you wouldn't know that she handles that part of the business too.

The items that sell the best at estate sales are antiques, paintings, jewelry, books, home furnishings, china, glass, fishing equipment, knickknacks, tools, local ephemera, kitchenware, local history pieces, advertising memorabilia, silver, and the like. In other words, anything valuable, in good condition, or in working order, such as appliances, will sell at estate sales, especially to neighbors or relatives who want a memento of the deceased.

TIP: Ed Tuten III, owner of Team Estate Sales located in Memphis, Tennessee, offers his services to seniors who are downsizing. He has an interior decorator on staff that helps to arrange their new apartments, as well as "broom clean" the old house. Real estate agents often request his services because more people are likely to see the house during the estate sale than any other day.

IN SUMMARY

So you've read about the pros and cons of selling your treasures through the experts. Whether you decide to enlist a prestigious auction house or a local auctioneer, you'll know what to expect. If you don't want to sit in a shop seven days a week or lug your goodies back and forth to a show, consignment and group shops are satisfying alternatives. If an entire estate falls your way, you can enlist the knowledge of an estate sale specialist or an auctioneer to take care of all the details of selling and disposing of nonsalable items as well. The next chapter will give you more opportunities to go it alone and broaden your selling horizons with eBay, shows, flea markets, single-shop ownership, and garage sales.

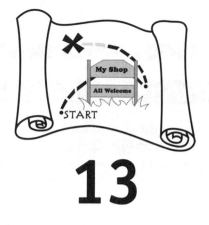

13

Selling Your Treasures on Your Own

You've accumulated a great deal of merchandise at yard sales or auctions, and now you want to sell your treasures. If you don't use an expert, as discussed in Chapter 12, you can strike out on your own. This chapter will briefly examine the pluses and minuses of selling your new-found treasures on your own.

Try one or several of the selling methods mentioned to discover what appeals to you. If you're not sure where to begin, base your selling techniques on

- Your personality type (type A—auctioneer or show seller; type B—eBay seller; and type C—consignment seller.)
- The merchandise you have (Knickknacks do well at flea markets or consignment shops.)
- The time of year (If you have a collection of holiday items, sell seasonally.)
- Your time commitment (If you have another job, having your own shop is not too feasible.)

As you study the marketplace and the types of goods you purchase, you will gain a better understanding of or a gut instinct for which items will sell on eBay, which items should go to a flea market, and which items need to remain in the closet until your next garage sale. Many dealers I know in the business have their own shop, sell at shows, and also do eBay. Of course, they are in the business full time. You have to find what works for you, and that will come only with trial and error, experience, and time.

When it comes to selling your goods yourself, there are several marketplaces to explore. As I've mentioned, you have to find which technique—or combination of techniques—is best for you. I'll go over each method in this

THE GRASS ISN'T ALWAYS GREENER

Dick and Jan heard how great eBay was and how much money all their friends made, so they sold off some of Dick's tool collection, and they had some pretty good scores. However, they soon found that it was easier to set up at shows and sell their merchandise in one weekend rather than to answer a ton of e-mails and pack and ship items they sold on eBay. Now they are much happier selling at shows five or six times a year than listing items for sale on eBay every week. The moral of the story is that you have to find what works for you.

chapter. Basically, the following are possible selling avenues that you can do yourself, and all of these are discussed in this chapter.

- Antique shop (single owner)
- Antique show or flea market
- eBay
- Garage or yard sale
- Miscellaneous (classified ads, bartering, private sale)

I'M DREAMING OF AN ANTIQUE SHOP

You've always dreamed of owning your own business, setting your own hours, and being your own boss; however, take heed. Much time and effort are required to make a go of it. A partnership is possible; just make sure that all the legal paperwork is drawn up so that everything is fair and that one person isn't left with all the bills and shop inventory if the other partner leaves or has a misfortune. A shop that is attached to your home has certain tax advantages, so you may want to consider that as an option. See the tax section in Chapter 14 for details on tax deductions.

Another consideration is the type of shop you'd like to operate. Are you going to have a junk shop with a wide variety of reasonable merchandise, or are you going to have an upscale store with high-end antiques and collectibles? The location of your shop, your budget, and your resources all will play a factor in your decision. Una Smith's shop, Granite Hill Antiques, in Westerly, Rhode Island, is located near the shore. She has to tailor her items seasonally because of her changing clientele. In the summer she sells more big-ticket items because her clients are from New York. In the winter she sells more knickknacks and giftware to the local residents.

To boost your profits as a shop owner, you can offer customers the option to consign pieces to your shop or list their valuables on eBay for a commission. Have a self-service coffee station with goodies so that customers will linger. For higher traffic flow and diverse customers, have a new gift room with crafts and candles or a room full of fine European imports adjacent to your antique shop; not everyone wants to buy old things. If you're really ambitious, open up your home as a bed and breakfast with an antique shop on the main floor.

Three schools of thought exist on how to arrange your merchandise—either in (1) an attractive and accessible manner, (2) like categories, or (3) chaotically so people have to search in every nook and cranny.

The Pros of Selling Out of Your Own Shop
- You are the boss and owner.
- You can hire or not hire help.
- You can set your own flexible shop hours.
- You can combine businesses (e.g., a bed and breakfast).
- You will get leads and contacts from people who visit.

The Cons of Selling Out of Your Own Shop
- If you don't sell out of your house or your barn, the rent could be a deterrent.
- If you're not at the shop during business hours, you have to find a trusted employee.
- You need a continuous supply of fresh merchandise.
- You are subject to the weather, such as snowstorms, resulting in lower sales that day.

TIP: Don't get greedy and wait too long to sell an item. If you price items too high, those items will sit in your shop and collect dust instead of collecting interest in your bank account.

MAKE YOURSELF AT HOME

Annette Branche owned an antique shop for 15 years in Mystic, Connecticut. She said that she loved having a shop because she loved to talk. She'd offer her customers "a couch and a cappuccino." More often than not, they would buy something from her because they felt comfortable. Therefore, if you have the gift of gab and enjoy company, maybe your own shop is the way to branch out!

ANTIQUE SHOW OR FLEA MARKET

Because these two categories are so similar, I have grouped them together. At an antique show or flea market, you sell your antiques to dealers, collectors, and the general buying public at a specified location on a certain day and time. The differences between a show and a flea market are based on booth rental and quality of merchandise. Booth rentals at prime shows are in the hundreds of dollars, whereas most flea market booths are under $100 and as low as $10 per table. Many shows are strictly high-class antiques and museum-quality merchandise, otherwise known as *high-end shows.* Flea markets consist of more general merchandise and junk, including edible products and "new in the box" items. However, there is a crossover in shows and flea markets where some shows accept more flea market–type items. Yet, for both antique shows and flea markets, the principles of selling are the same.

The Pros of Selling at a Show or Flea Market
- Avid collectors search out specialty items.
- People come from a wide variety of places.
- Your sales personality will sell the item.

The Cons of Selling at a Show or Flea Market
- You are often in the hands of Mother Nature (at outdoor shows and flea markets).
- You have to wrap, pack, load, and unload at least four times for a one-day show.
- Your sales could suffer owing to poor advertising, attendance, or the economy.

TRUE DIEHARDS!

Marylynne and her husband, Conrad, set up at the Brimfield Antique Show (an open field) in Brimfield, Massachusetts, one September when a tornado was forecasted for the area. Most dealers packed up and never returned. Marylynne and Conrad lugged their Victorian furniture and glassware into the center of their space and secured everything with a tarp and bungie cords. They rode out the storm, and neither they nor their merchandise were harmed. They never gave up the ship and that week their ship came in and they had a very profitable show.

Which Show Is a Go?

To start selling at shows or flea markets, ask the dealers when you go to other shows which shows they prefer. Who runs a good show? Who is fair? Who has reasonable costs? What shows draw the crowds? Shows are listed in the calendar sections of antique journals and newspapers. There are several books on the market that list flea markets all over the country, such as *U.S. Flea Market Directory* and *Official Directory to U.S. Flea Markets*. Go to the Web and type in www.fleamarketguide.com. From there you can click on a state and get a listing of flea markets in that state. Go to any online bookstore and search under books for more information. Go to the Web and type in "[your state] and antique shows," and a useful listing will appear. Phone numbers and Web sites of particular shows will be listed. Call up the manager or show promoter to see if space is available and to get the rates. You may have to send in a deposit to hold your space. Many flea markets and shows already have contracted spaces for "regulars." Regulars set up every week for the contracted time, say, 9 or 12 months.

If you want to sell at a show or a flea market, call up the management and ask the following questions:

- *May I reserve a space?* Some places let you reserve ahead; some places make you wait until that morning for a space.
- *What size is your space, and how much does it cost?* This varies from state to state and location to location. Flea markets generally are cheaper. Shows vary depending on location and number of days. Regulars may get a discounted rate if they sell at one show for the contracted time.
- *What happens in the event of rain?* You need to know if you should bring a tarp or your umbrella and whether or not you are charged a penalty if you are a no-show.
- *Do I need my own tables?* Some flea markets will rent out tables for a slight charge on a first-come basis.
- *What time do I arrive to unload?* Setup begins early, such as 5 to 7 A.M., so plan your time accordingly.
- *May I use my car or van as part of the space or move my vehicle somewhere else after I unload?* This will give you an idea of how many tables you need.
- *What time may I start packing up?* Some organizations request that you stay a full day and not leave when the crowds thin out.

On arrival at the show or flea market, someone will direct you to your location. If they don't collect the booth money on the spot, someone from management will come around to each booth and collect your fee, including the fee for any rented tables you requested.

Essential Equipment for a Show or Flea Market

You can try to cram everything into your car, but unless you know that you can rent tables, try to borrow a friend's truck or van. Price items and load them into your vehicle the night before because setup time is usually early in the morning, and you may have to drive a distance.

Some of the equipment you will need to set up at a show are several 8-foot tables, a few card tables, portable stacking shelves to display items, plate stands for china, tablecloths, a chair for you, and an umbrella or tarp if you are outside. If you have an electric outlet, spotlights are a great selling technique to liven up your merchandise. Also have on hand extra stickers and tags in case some stickers fall off or you want to change your prices. For jewelry or small items, have a loop, magnifying glass, or tape measure available for your customers.

For sales, a carbonless receipt book is necessary (available at office supply stores) if someone wants a receipt for a purchase. A cash box (tucked away in a corner near your seat) or money belt is important. Have empty boxes and paper and plastic bags available to wrap small purchases. Brown paper lunch bags or small baggies are great for jewelry or small knickknacks.

TIP: You will do 80 percent of your selling for the day before the gates open to the public. Let the dealers buy while you unload. Everything doesn't have to be unwrapped or perfectly displayed for you to make a sale.

Tricks of the Trade

To get people to stop at your booth, try the following:

- Display a showstopper (see Figure 13-1). You don't necessarily have to sell that item, but it will magnetize people to your booth.
- Keep the best merchandise at eye level. Not everyone bends down and looks under tables and in boxes.
- If your booth is inside, spotlight your best pieces, such as good glass or jewelry, in showcases.
- Have items that appeal to both men and women if you aren't specializing in one area.
- Dress the part. If you sell vintage clothing, wear a vintage hat. If you sell vintage jewelry, wear an unusual pin. This can open a conversation and close a sale.
- Have mirrors in your booth for sale. The booth appears larger, people can try something on, and you could sell the mirror too.

Figure 13-1   A showstopper such as this replica of King Tut's sarcophagus will attract people to your booth.

- Have plenty of your business cards in view, especially if you have a shop or a Web site or specialize in a certain area.
- Have free merchandise, such as pens or fans, with your name on them (free advertising).

eBAY THE EASY WAY

Many books are available regarding selling on eBay. If you're really interested in trying your hand at eBay, find a mentor and also read Dennis Prince's book, *How to Sell Anything on eBay and Make a Fortune*.

The number of registered users on eBay grows daily. People have a worldwide market where they can sell cars, boats, real estate, antiques, giftware, and hundreds of other categories. Does this sound too good to be true? As with all selling options I've mentioned, pros and cons to this method need to be weighed also.

WHAT COLOR IS MY TABLECLOTH?

Barbara Lee-Roberts, a successful flea marketeer known by her business name as Spice...s Nice, finds that certain colored tablecloths work to her advantage when she sells at flea markets. She says that anything will sell on pink. Pink means love, and people are very open to that color. She uses brown tweed to make brass and copper stand out and to make antiques look older. Black works well with jewelry and newer items. She advises against using red or white because (1) "red means stop and stop means don't buy me" and (2) white gives off too much glare in the sun. Barbara also recommends getting a corner or end space at a flea market for more visibility and traffic flow and thus more sales.

The Pros of Selling on eBay
- You can set your own hours (you can list items at two in the morning if you can't sleep).
- You can preenter all the information, and for a miniscule charge, you can designate what day you want the item to get posted.
- You can place a reserve on an item (a reserve is a minimum value that you are willing to let the item sell for).
- Your item, once listed, is sold in seven days or less.
- You can set up your own eBay store as another outlet to sell your merchandise.
- If you're shy, you don't ever have to talk to or meet anyone in person.
- You will meet and often acquire friends worldwide.

TIP: You can see how many hits or number of people visit each item you list on eBay by adding a free counter to keep track.

The Cons of Selling on eBay
- You may have to deal with unsatisfied customers (some who will be unsatisfied no matter what you do and want their money back).
- You may have to wait 7 to 10 days for a personal check to clear.
- You may have to relist items that don't sell the first time around.
- You may end up in the packing and shipping business.

A RECORD NUMBER OF VISITORS

On eBay you can have 1, 100, or 1,000 people look at and bid on your item. Glenn listed a 25-year-old John Deere riding lawnmower on eBay one spring, and 2,600 people visited his site. This would never happen in your shop, not in a week. Ironically, the lawnmower sold to a man in the next town.

- You may not sell anything one week.
- If you list something unreserved and let it go for 99 cents, it could sell for 99 cents.

TIP: If you discover that packing peanuts and slicing up cardboard boxes is not your style, hire a high school student to help you after school.

FIVE SIMPLE STEPS TO SELL YOUR FIRST ITEM ON eBAY

So you want to try your hand at selling one of the items you picked up for a few bucks. You will need a

- Computer
- Digital camera
- Credit card
- Checking account
- Packing material
- Boxes and labels

Step 1: Register at eBay

Go to the net and type in www.ebay.com. When the home page is visible, you can click on "Register Now." This is the process:

1. You have to enter personal information such as where you live, your phone number, your date of birth, and your e-mail address and create your user ID and a password.
2. You have to agree to eBay's user terms and privacy policy that you can read immediately and print out.
3. Check your e-mail for registration confirmation.

TIP: Having trouble creating a user ID because that user ID is already taken? eBay will help you if you give the company three categories it can work with, such as your hobby, a color, and an animal. For example, *antiques, silver,* and *cat* becomes *silvercatantiques* as a user ID.

Step 2: Create a Seller's Account

If you're already an eBay user, your user ID will appear, and you only need to log in your password. If you do not have a seller's account, you have to

1. Verify the information you entered.
2. Provide identification (this is on a secure site).
   a. A credit or debit card (this is how eBay bills you for services you use) and
   b. A checking account number (this gives eBay verification of your identity and increases safety).
3. Select how to pay seller fees.
   a. Deduct eBay seller fees from your checking account or
   b. Charge eBay seller fees to your credit card.

In about 30 seconds, if everything goes through, you will get a congratulations notice, and you can now sell on eBay.

TIP: Be aware of false e-mails known as "spoof" e-mails that are disguised as urgent messages from eBay asking for your credit card and personal information. Don't give any information out. Only provide that kind of e-mail directly through the eBay Web site. If you think a spoof is in the works, you can file a report with eBay. On the bottom of eBay's home page, click on "Security Center," and then click on "Report a Problem."

Step 3: List Your Item

Once you've created a seller's account, you can sell immediately or return at a later time to eBay's home page and click on "Sell Your Item." You then will be guided to sell your item in five easy steps: (1) Select a category, (2) give a title and description, (3) include pictures and details, (4) enter payment and shipping information, and (5) review and submit your listing.

Once you've accomplished these steps, you will be assigned a number for your item, which you will use in all your correspondence. Step 3, which is really five steps within this step, may take you 20 minutes. You can cut down this time if you write your title and description and shoot your photos ahead of time. It still takes time to do this, but you will be able to upload more items in an hour if some of the prework is already done.

TIP: A "gallery" photo is a must if you want customers to click on your item and read further. See Figure 13-2 for examples. A gallery photo costs 25 cents and is well worth the price. This is the first picture people see if they do a search and type in a particular item. Often the gallery photo and title you use will determine whether that person clicks on your site and bids. Sometimes eBay runs specials on the cost of gallery photos, so do your listing then.

Step 4: Contact Your Buyer

When the auction process is over and your item has sold, you will be sent an e-mail notice. You are then instructed to contact the buyer to make payment

☐	click here to see the picture	Old Metal Hubley Toy Truck 🖂♡	$19.99	-	2d 17h 12m
☐	📷	1957 Toy Catalog Buddy L Tonka Nylint Marx Eldon Hubley	$19.95	1	8d 02h 06m
☐	📷	Hubley P-40 Flying Circus Toy Metal Airplane P40 Plane 🖂♡	$19.50	5	12m
☐	📷	Hubley Kiddie Toy Truck, 452, vintage Toy 1950 🖂♡	$19.00	-	18h 05m
☐	ything toys Clive & Toni	🔨 HUBLEY KIDDIE-TOY : Vintage diecast Racing Car 🖂♡	GBP 9.99	-	4d 22h 32m
☐	🚗	5 OLD TOY Car Cars Cast Iron Metal USA Hubley Tootie 🖂♡	$16.49	2	4d 23h 11m
☐	🏍	1950s HUBLEY Kiddie Toy 5in. Plastic Motorcycle Toy 🖂♡	$15.99 ≡Buy It Now	-	3d 01h 06m
☐	🔫	🔨 1930's Hubley Cowboy Western Style Toy Cap Gun Pistol 🖂♡	$15.00	-	6d 18h 32m
☐	📷	HUBLEY KIDDY TOY -#4-FOR PARTS-	$15.00	-	2d 00h 07m

Figure 13-2 A gallery photo on eBay often determines whether a customer will click on your listing or someone else's.

and shipping arrangements. eBay will deduct the listing and selling fees automatically from your credit card and bill you monthly. To find out what the fees are, you can click on "Selling," then on "Listing Your Item," and finally on "Fees." An overview and six pages of fees pop up.

In a nutshell, insertion fees are based on the starting price of your item, that is, 30 cents for an item listed from 1 to 99 cents. The price increases from there. Final value fees are based on the final sale price of your item, that is, 5.25 percent of the closing value from \$0 to \$25. And again, the percentage increases from there.

Step 5: Ship the Merchandise

After the buyer sends payment and his funds clear your bank, you can then ship out the merchandise. Send the merchandise and a receipt to the buyer. Ask the buyer once he has received the merchandise and is satisfied with the transaction to leave you feedback comments. This adds to your reputation and selling power on eBay.

TIP: Sellers who achieve high volumes of monthly sales and receive a positive feedback rating of 98 percent or better are invited to participate in the eBay PowerSeller program. Members enjoy certain promotional offers and opportunities. Membership is free, but you must maintain a certain level of monthly sales and feedback rating. Go to eBay's home page and click on "Services," and then scroll down to "Advanced Seller Services" and click on "PowerSeller Program."

Recommendations for a Successful eBay Sale

- If you think that you have a one-of-a-kind item, do a search on eBay. If 50 other like items are already listed, wait a week or two before you list your item.
- Always answer your e-mails, no matter how ridiculous the question (the person took the time to e-mail you; offer the same courtesy).
- Take the time to write an interesting story about the item you're selling.
- Don't skimp on your pictures (the first one is free; you can spring for three or four more or buy a "Picture Pack" offered by eBay—up to 6 pictures for \$1.00 or 7 to 12 pictures for \$1.50).
- Take clear, crisp pictures of an item without other distractions in the background unless those props will help sell the item (see Figure 13-3).
- Once someone is a successful bidder, contact the person immediately

(eBay gives you three days, but why wait? The sooner you respond, the sooner you get your money).

- Consider using PayPal. This is an eBay Company that lets you send and receive payments online using credit cards. You must apply for the premier/business account to receive credit card payments and fees of 1.9 to 2.9 percent, plus 30 cents applies. Please note that customers expect their items to be shipped sooner than if they send payment through the mail.

Getting to Know You

There are a number of ways a potential bidder can get to know you on eBay. Take advantage of all these areas to increase bidder potential. The prominent ones are

- Feedback
- All About Me
- eBay Store

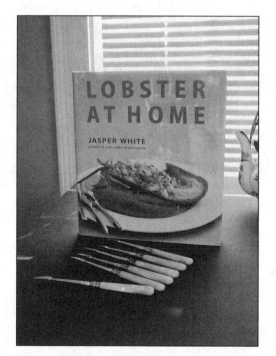

Figure 13-3   eBay PowerSeller Clark van der Lyke known as williams712 on eBay added a lobster book as a backdrop to entice buyers to bid on an everyday set of lobster (nut) picks.

Feedback

The number one thing that keeps every seller in check on eBay is known as "Feedback." Any buyer can leave feedback regarding a seller or the item that she purchased. Feedback is a line or two and a rating such as "Great item, courteous service, quick shipping A+A+A+A+." A seller with 100 percent feedback generally means that the customers are satisfied with the seller, his item, his description, his quick shipping, and his courtesy. Anyone who is thinking of buying from a seller should go into the feedback history and read about that particular seller. Be leery of buying from anyone who has a low feedback rating.

TIP: "If something has a chip, crack, or damage," says Barbara van der Lyke of Arts and Antiques on College Hill, "we tell them. Honesty is the best policy. We tell the customer if the item's not what you want, we will gladly refund your money. We've never had to do that in six years."

All About Me

To have people bid on your site, they might feel more comfortable if they could read a short history about you. Tell them how you got started in the business, what you buy, and your hobbies. Include terms of sale, feedback comments, and items up for bid. You don't need a degree in Web design to accomplish this. To set up an "All About Me" page, go to eBay's home page and click on "Services," and then click on "Member Reputation—About Me page." Once your page is completed, a small "me" icon appears next to your user ID on your eBay site.

eBay Store

Another variation of selling on eBay is the eBay Store. The store consists of customized pages created by you that talk about your business and list your items for sale. You also can include other items that aren't anywhere else on eBay, such as fixed price ("Buy It Now") items. A monthly subscription fee applies ($15.95 per month for basic service). Insertion fees are 2 cents per 30 days, and final value fees for store inventory are 8 percent of the closing value from $0 to $25. A small "red tag" icon (signifying that you have an eBay store) appears next to your name when someone clicks onto your eBay site.

TIP: To search for a particular seller on eBay, click on Advanced Search" in the upper right of eBay's home page. Then look under Find Items and click on "Items by seller. A screen will appear and you will be prompted to type in the seller's user id, such as "kats4dog11" or "muffstuff."

YOUR OWN GARAGE OR YARD SALE

Is eBay too mind-boggling, and are computers too technical? Do you have an accumulation of stuff that's not really worthy of a fine antique show? Do you just want to turn over items once or twice a year without having to commit to the time and money needed for a shop? Do you have good intentions of going to the consignment shop but never make the phone call? Then perhaps having your own garage sale, either alone or in conjunction with your neighbors, is the best route to take.

TIP: To know how to price items for a garage sale, visit other garage or yard sales. Books, clothing, toys, and pots and pans are easy to price. If you have a valuable antique, do your homework by checking on eBay, looking in a price guide, or getting an expert's opinion.

The Pros of Having Your Own Garage or Yard Sale
- You know that the event is going to happen on a certain day, and you can plan accordingly.
- For a garage sale, you don't have to worry about weather.
- For a yard sale, you can schedule a rain date.
- Team up with others in the neighborhood for a multineighborhood sale.
- Gear your sale to be an annual event.

The Cons of Having Your Own Garage or Yard Sale
- Strangers will scope out your property.
- A crowd may descend on you at the crack of dawn.
- Your sale may bomb if you are too far out in the "boonies."
- Other events in the area may draw people away from your sale.
- You may have only lookers if your items aren't desirable or if they are priced too high.
- You may not get as much money for an item because people at yard sales are usually looking for bargains.

Hints For a Fabulous Garage or Yard Sale

You might have a good yard sale with little or no effort, but to have a fabulous yard sale where you will maximize your profits, you need to plan at least a month or more in advance. The following hints not only will make the day less stressful but also will make it enjoyable and profitable as well.

Before the Sale
Preparation time is needed to put the sale together. You should

- Get organized. Designate one room in your house or one bay of your garage for the upcoming sale.
- Sort and place like items together for easier pricing.
- Ask neighbors or relatives if they want to have a neighborhood sale or a multifamily sale.
- Advertise well through local newspapers, posters, and notices on community bulletin boards.
- Have clear directions in your ad and secured, bold-colored signs on route to your sale.
- Price items in advance of the sale, not the morning of the sale.
- Leave room in the price for haggling because most dealers and early birds want a discount.
- Get a permit, if needed, from the town or city.
- Check on the rules if you live in a gated community or trailer park. They may not allow any yard sales or restrict the number of sales you can have in a year.
- Check with the town as to rules on placement of signs. (In my town, you're not allowed to place any signs within 50 feet of the historical center.)
- Have plenty of small bills and change on hand (at least $100, with $50 in ones and a roll of quarters and dimes).
- Hire friends or relatives to help display, sell, and clean up.
- Have most of the sale already set up and accented with spotlights if you're having your sale in the garage.

TIP: Advertise in a newspaper that promotes, "Free Yard Sale Kit." These handy kits usually include preprinted signs and arrows, price tags, inventory and tip sheet, and a marking pen.

AND THE SIGN SAID

John had moved to a new location on a cul-de-sac only streets away from his old house, and his yearly yard sales seemed to gross less than in previous years. John discovered that less traffic passed by his new road. He remedied this by placing three or four different colored signs at the end of the street suggesting more than one sale in the neighborhood.

Sale Day

Many details need to be handled on sale day. The number one rule is to dele-
gate responsibility. You should have

- Help. Don't think you can do it all yourself, especially if this is your
  first sale.
- A smile for those early birds who want to buy first. If you're ready for
  them, let them buy; this is better than losing a sale.
- Someone willing to put out signs early. You can distribute directional
  signs the night before, but if you don't use permanent ink, your let-
  tering may smear from the dew, or the signs may disappear mysteri-
  ously.
- Relatives who arrive early to help display items outside if the weather
  is nice.
- An area for empty boxes, newspapers, and plastic bags for the cus-
  tomers.
- A coffee and donut or lemonade stand if you have kids and they
  want to help.
- A separate cashout area with a calculator.
- A pad or receipt book and pens to write down sales.
- A cashier at the cash box at all times.
- A fanny pack to tuck away larger bills.
- Someone to check halfway through the sale that the signs are still up
  in the community.
- Someone to take down the signs after the sale.
- Helpers to bring items back inside that didn't sell.

Successful Display Techniques to Sell Your Goods

To maximize your profits, you need to maximize the appeal to drivers-by and
lookers. The following techniques are recommended by Kathrina Glass from
Minnesota who holds successful yard sales twice-yearly:

- Place furniture and tools out near the road, so men will stop.
- Place a fancy woman's dress or colorful quilt out front, so women
  will stop.
- Put 5- by 7-inch signs in front of a group of items, such as "Videos
  $2.00 each" or "This table—$1.00 choice."
- If there is a lull in shoppers, fold clothes, rearrange your tables, and
  fill in any gaps.
- Label all sets as to size—such as sheets (twin, double, queen, or
  king).

- If you don't hang up clothes, safety pin any sets together and fold them neatly.
- Arrange similar glass and china together on velvet or flashy table-cloths.
- If you have numerous pictures and mirrors, bang nails into the walls and display them, or if your space is limited, line pictures face up in a large cardboard box for easy flip-through motion.
- Use jumbo baggies to keep toys, puzzles, and games together, and write "Complete" on the outside of the bag along with the price.
- Use spotlights to accent glassware or jewelry that is displayed in a showcase.

TIP: Kathrina Glass also recommends hanging clothes by size categories on a clothes rack. If you don't have one, Kathrina says an extension ladder or a swing set works well (see Figure 13-4). She also recommends placing a kids' toy bin near the clothing so that parents can keep an eye on their kids and look at clothes at the same time.

Figure 13-4 An old swing set is the perfect display rack for clothing.

MISCELLANEOUS SELLING CATEGORIES

To start with, you may not have enough merchandise for a flea market or show. Or you may not be physically fit to move furniture in and out of your truck five times. If you only have one or two items to sell, try something a little less stressful.

Here are a few more ways to sell your goods:

- Classified ads
- Weekly "Bargain Hunter" booklets
- Bartering
- Private sales

Classified Ads

Do you have only a handful of items to sell? Place an ad in the classified section of your local newspaper (the rate is usually by the word). Give a few lines of description; include your phone number and the best time to call. Some newspapers have "Bargain Bin" sections where you can advertise for free. Just call your local paper to find out details about how to do this.

"Bargain Hunter" Booklets

These weekly booklets such as *The WANT ADvertiser* or *Uncle Henry's Weekly Swap or Sell It Guide* list all kinds of merchandise for sale, including real estate, boats, RV's, cars, fishing equipment, sports equipment, musical instruments, and so on. This is a good place not only to sell items but also to buy items. These booklets usually are placed in local drugstores or grocery stores and are fairly inexpensive. See the Resources section for addresses and Web sites.

Bartering

This is a term used to exchange one type of merchandise or collectible for another item of equal value. Many collectors in the trade will (1) swap items where no money is exchanged, (2) barter and exchange money, or (3) trade for an item. When you buy at shows or shops, ask people if they are willing to barter with you; some will, and some will not. Some of the swap guides list items for sale by barter. Or go to the Web and type in www.barter.net. This company lists numerous Web sites of companies that barter anything, such as boats, cars, antiques, computers, art, tools, and real estate.

Private Sales

Word-of-mouth advertising, contacts, and leads from other people will give you a good base clientele for private sales. Private buyers may collect the types of items that you sell and will pay top dollar to add these specialty items to their collection. The object is to search for items for that particular person and then sell to her privately. Your overhead is low. There is no middleman to work through, and you can keep your own "little black book" of best customers and their collecting habits.

DEALER'S CHOICE

Whatever method of selling you use, it's up to you. You may have a gut instinct to sell something through a big auction house. You may find that eBay is the type of flexible business you desire. You may like the one-on-one contact with other people and prefer to have your own shop. You may like the hustle and excitement of setting up at flea markets and shows. You may be more conservative and only want to place an ad in the paper when you find something valuable. Whatever you do, be assured that someone will knock on your shop door, bid on your eBay site, scope out your yard sale, or call you on the phone to buy your treasure because now the shoe is on the other foot, and they are searching for that bargain or special piece to add to their collection.

14

Taking the Plunge: Building a Business with Your Treasures

So you've had a taste of making a garage sale find and selling a treasure at an auction. You've made a substantial hit or a few little hits that add up to a big sum of money, and you think that this is easy. Sit down and count to 10. Too many people want instant gratification, and you may achieve that momentarily with a big hit, but before you give up your day job, consider the financial and time commitment that it will take to build your business and become successful.

The best advice is to start small but think big. If you're going to take the plunge, stick your big toe in first and then both feet to feel the water rather than diving off, doing a belly flop, and going into shock because the water is too cold. Statistics show that most small business fail within the first five years. Take it slow; you'll get there soon enough.

THE PASSION INGREDIENT

A key to this (or any other business) is that you have to love what you do. Are you willing to give up your weekends and some weeknights to poke through boxes at auctions? Are you willing to travel long distances to set up at shows in the pouring rain? Are you willing to drive around and beat others to area yard sales? Are you willing to write flowery descriptions and take digital photos of items to sell on eBay? You don't have to eat, sleep, and breathe auctions and flea markets and eBay, but in all honesty, it certainly helps.

Jeff Izzo, a dealer from Connecticut who likes to be known as "passionately connected" to the business, maintains that, "It's all about networking with other people. It's not about the money; it's just that I love the business and the people in it."

Meg Whitman, chief executive officer (CEO) of eBay, suggested in an interview on "Good Morning America" that you have to have a passion for what you sell. If she had time, she would sell antique fly-fishing items. Another woman from Portland, Maine, had a passion for vintage clothing and made $20,000 a year profit. And a husband and wife team outside of Chicago loved selling tools and machinery. They bought their house from their profits on eBay. It can be done. Do you have the passion to do it?

CHOOSING YOUR PROFESSION

Now you have to decide, "What will I be when I grow up?" I never had to decide because I was only 12 years old when I became an auctioneer and was selling to hundreds of people on the auction block. You might say that I grew up in a family auction business, or you might say that I never grew up. Either way, I love what I do. So think about what you would love to do if you've already had a small taste of success in this business. You have a few choices or a combination of choices that may work for you. You could become an

- Auctioneer/appraiser
- Antique dealer/shop owner
- eBay PowerSeller

You could combine all the above if you're ambitious and energetic and have the time to devote to the business. However, I would suggest that you ease into a new career on a part-time basis. The great advantage of these occupations is that you *can* start on the weekends or at night, and eventually, if your business grows and you're successful, you can think about going full time.

Who'll Bid $2,500 for It? Life as an Auctioneer

To become an auctioneer, you have choices too:

1. *Work under another licensed auctioneer.* Apprenticeship or references are required in some states to get your license.
2. *Go to auction school.* These schools are located throughout the country and are usually only a one- or two-week course. The courses are reasonably priced, and they are offered at different times throughout the year. You can find information by doing a search on the Web or by contacting the National Auctioneers Association in Overland Park, Kansas.
3. *Hang out your sign and start with no formal training.* You will soon discover the difference between the professional and the amateur auctioneer, and you may want to shoot for professionalism.

Most states do not require formal training, and not all states require an auctioneer's license. The states that require a license also require that you register yearly and pay a fee. Check with the division of standards in your state for licensing laws and fees.

Deal Me In: Becoming an Antique Dealer

To become an antique dealer, you again need to register with the state and get a resale number for your business. This is so that you don't pay tax on items that you're going to resell. Some states have no sales tax, so you don't have to worry. However, many people I know in the business don't bother to get a tax number; they pay the tax instead. They find this way easier than filling out piles of paperwork and signing a form at each new auction or shop in which they buy. Every state is different regarding tax numbers. Some states will not accept other state sales tax numbers, so you must have one for that particular state if you buy there. But once you register with the state, it will send you a resale tax certificate with an identification number.

A misconception is that a dealer has to physically own a shop. You can freelance your merchandise to auctions and consignment stores, rent dealer space in a group shop, or open a virtual store on eBay. Kim May of Kimamay the eBay Way! doesn't own her own shop but instead sells out of 18 spaces in four states. This frees up her time to buy antiques, attend shows, be a Power-Seller on eBay, and maintain an eBay store.

TIP: Your tax number is only valid on items that you're going to buy and resell, not on items for personal use.

Internet Power

To become an eBay seller, reread the section on eBay in Chapter 13. To become an eBay PowerSeller, you have to meet certain criteria with regard to feedback percentages and monthly gross sales.

ALL THINGS CONSIDERED

Some of the factors that you will need to consider when you go into business are

- Startup capital (It takes money to make money.)
- Startup costs (rent, inventory, advertising, employees)
- Family obligations (If you're single, you may have more freedom than if you have family commitments.)
- Taxes (The Internal Revenue Service wants its share of your treasures.)
- Ethics (moral and immoral issues to think about)

STARTUP CAPITAL

If you didn't win the lottery or inherit some money from your rich uncle, you will have to set aside some money or take out a home equity loan before you can start your business. Startup costs are numerous and can include education (auction school or appraiser's course), licenses (state and town for businesses), rent (for a shop), advertising (to get the word out, brochures, business cards, Web page), inventory (antiques or household furnishings for your shop), sound systems and computer programs (for auctions), employees (either hired or subcontracted), and taxes (money to be paid monthly, quarterly, or yearly). Here are a few costs to consider:

Inventory

In this business, if you plan to expand beyond a weekend hobby, you have to have enough cash flow to buy inventory and still make a profit. Build slowly if that's all you can afford. Experiment to see what works best for you and your wallet. You may be able to do it all yourself, or you may need to hire someone reliable to keep shop hours while you go out and buy. However, if you hire employees, all kinds of taxes apply, such as worker's compensation, withholding, state taxes, and more, so make sure that you are financially ready for that part of the business.

Another important aspect of business success is to devise some type of system to keep track of inventory (especially for tax purposes, which I talk about later in this chapter). You don't have to get fancy. You don't need a computer or spreadsheet program, although it is easier and less time-consuming if you have one. Basically, for each item, you want to list the date of purchase, the amount you paid, the code or inventory number you assign to it, when it sold, how much it sold for, shipping charges, and your profit.

Some dealers have devised certain letters that correspond with certain numbers, and by looking at that code, they can tell how much they paid for an item and what amount they can deduct for a dealer discount. Other dealers also will use a three-letter abbreviation for the location where they bought an entire house. For example, a friend of mine uses a different letter for the numbers 1 through 10 to code what she paid for an item so that she can deduct a small amount if someone asks for a discount. The words *buy me right* are easy to remember. Thus, if she paid $25 for something, the code on her tag would read "UE." You can get more elaborate if you want and include a letter or number where you bought the item and the date you bought it also.

B	U	Y	M	E	R	I	G	H	T
1	2	3	4	5	6	7	8	9	10

BE IN TUNE

Toby Castle started buying and selling one musical instrument at a time because that's all he could afford. His mode of operation is exemplified in his business name, The One Man Band. Now, five years later, he can afford to buy an entire orchestra because he built his business up one step at a time and didn't go for all the frills and extras that you can get caught up in when you first open a business.

It's All in a Name

Advertising is an essential part of anyone's business growth. Choosing a name is sometimes a difficult task. For example, when my dad first started out in the business, he named his company after his auction barn, The Whiffletree Auction Gallery. Someone in business told him, "No one's going to remember that name; use your own name." My dad followed that advice and used his own name—Robert H. Glass Auctioneers & Appraisers. Over the years, his impeccable reputation and his name became synonymous.

I already discussed names to use on eBay and how eBay can help you to come up with a user ID name. These names can relate to your specialty so that people know that's what you sell, such as "chinagirl" or "cameraman," or the names can imply a broader meaning, such as "auctioncellar" or "pacrat8."

Shop names can encompass a little more variety to attract people driving or walking by, such as Once in a Blue Moon Antiques or Never Say Goodbye Antiques. See Figure 14-1.

How Do I Advertise? Let Me Count the Ways!

Advertising is expensive, but here are seven simple ways to advertise

- *Free publicity.* Contact the local newspapers. They may run a feature story on you if you have an angle, connect your sales to charity, or sell something at auction that has local history.
- *Classified ads.* Run a classified ad every week in the newspaper to let customers know that you buy and sell items or that you have a shop. People will call or stop by. Classified advertising (located in the back of the paper) is certainly cheaper than display advertising (in other sections of the paper). Watch for special issues and rates that the newspapers will run so that you can advertise your business.
- *Business cards.* You can design and print your own business cards on your computer or go to Staples and choose a design and get 500

Figure 14-1 This antique shop on Martha's Vineyard is inviting because of its name and entrance display.

made. See Figure 14-2 for two examples. You can put these in your eBay packages when you ship goods. You can carry them with you to yard sales, flea markets, and shows or tack them up on community bulletin boards. If you're a member of an organization or have special skills, list that on your card to add to your authority and professionalism.

- *Newspaper column writing.* Explore the possibilities of writing an occasional article or an antiques column in a local or weekly newspaper. This is another free way to get your name known in the community. Try writing an article. You may become syndicated and get a readership following, or you may get a chance to buy an entire estate. Robert Glass wrote a weekly column entitled, "Searching the Antique Attic," for several years for a local newspaper. People sent him questions and photos of their treasures, and each week he would answer their questions, help identify collectibles, and give values on antiques. Often these people wanted to sell their items, and Robert would consign those items to his antique auctions.
- *Public speaking.* Offer to speak at local clubs such as a Rotary or Kiwanis Club or the local historical society or library. Most groups welcome the opportunity to have a speaker talk about special areas

Figure 14-2   Business cards are an inexpensive and valuable form of advertising.

of interest such as antiques, auctions, or collecting. Include a free appraisal when you become confident about giving estimated values on certain items. Helen Louth, owner of The Hope Chest in Johnston, Rhode Island, regularly conducts free appraisal days and is overwhelmed with people who have items not only for appraisals but for sale as well.

- *Web site.* Some of the programs you subscribe to on the Web will let you list a basic Web site. If your business would thrive on a Web site, such as an auction company, find someone to help you design one. It's not necessary when you first start out to spend thousands of dollars on a Web site.

- *Word of mouth.* This is free and the best form of advertising available. When other people suggest you for the job because of something you've done in the past, the accolades can only grow, and other people will call on you.

TIP: If someone is satisfied with your business transaction, have him write you a personal letter that you can put in your portfolio as a reference for future business.

- *Other forms.* Many other forms of advertising exist, and as you build your business, you can capitalize on these areas, such as direct mailings, brochures, radio, and cable TV.

All In the Family

Many of these businesses can involve an entire family. For example, in an auction business, one spouse could be the auctioneer. The other spouse could be the cashier. The aunt could run the computer system. Uncles and cousins could be assistants and hold up the merchandise for auction. The kids could run the food booth. The pet could be the security system or the "Watch Dog." Look to relatives, neighbors, and friends to help you get started.

THE TAX MAN COMETH

Taxes are inevitable, but with a little help, taxes do not have to be a foreign language. To make sure that the Internal Revenue Service (IRS) won't knock at your door, please consult an authority or tax accountant. Lisa Jeck, of Pensato, LLC, of New Boston, New Hampshire, a veteran in the tax business for 16 years, was consulted on the basic tax issues below.

Hobby or Business? That is the Question

Going to garage sales and auctions is a hobby if you are purchasing items for yourself and do not intend to make a profit. Thus, there is a limit on how many deductions you can declare. On the other hand, becoming an expert and spending time and education to develop this hobby where you make a profit results in a business. Taxes and deductions will be treated differently.

The Basic Tax Forms

Most people in this business will have a sole proprietorship, and your taxes will be part of your personal tax return. In other words, you will no longer be filing a 1040 EZ tax form. You have to break down and list separately your expenses, your profits, and your losses.

The most likely form you will need is the profit and loss form called a Schedule C (see Figure 14-3). Other forms include mileage, home office, and depreciation of assets you purchase such as computer or office equipment. If you have a profit from the business, you may have a self-employment tax form, which is the Social Security tax. All these forms can be downloaded from the IRS website at www.irs.gov.

Record Keeping

Is your heart palpitating, and are your palms sweaty? Don't worry. You can alleviate those tax anxieties by keeping accurate records. These records should

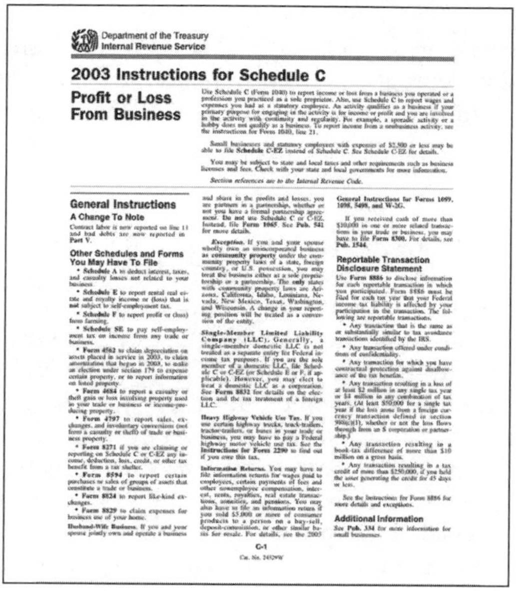
Department of the Treasury
Internal Revenue Service

2003 Instructions for Schedule C

Profit or Loss From Business

Use Schedule C (Form 1040) to report income or loss from a business you operated or a profession you practiced as a sole proprietor. Also, use Schedule C to report wages and expenses you had as a statutory employee. An activity qualifies as a business if your primary purpose for engaging in the activity is for income or profit and you are involved in the activity with continuity and regularity. For example, a sporadic activity or a hobby does not qualify as a business. To report income from a nonbusiness activity, see the instructions for Form 1040, line 21.

Small businesses and statutory employees with expenses of $2,500 or less may be able to file **Schedule C-EZ** instead of Schedule C. See Schedule C-EZ for details.

You may be subject to state and local taxes and other requirements such as business licenses and fees. Check with your state and local governments for more information.

Section references are to the Internal Revenue Code.

General Instructions

A Change To Note

Contract labor is now reported on line 11 and bad debts are now reported in Part V.

Other Schedules and Forms You May Have To File

Reportable Transaction Disclosure Statement

Additional Information

C-1

Figure 14-3 A sole proprietorship business most likely will file the profit and loss form called Schedule C.

be done on a monthly basis. If you are organized and meticulous, a weekly basis is even better.

TIP: Tax accountant Lisa Jeck recommends that you keep some form of records, either by hand or on a computer using an Excel spreadsheet or a bookkeeping program; QuickBooks and Peachtree are two suggestions. She prefers that your record keeping match your comfort level; the important thing is that you keep records on a regular basis.

Expense Deductions

You can deduct a number of expenses when you own your own business. These expenses will offset your profit margin and thus lower your taxes. A new law allows taxpayers to deduct up to $5,000 of startup costs in the year in which their business begins (effective after October 22, 2004). Please consult your tax accountant for clarification and further details. The most common deductions are highlighted as follows:

Inventory

Keep records on the inventory you buy and sell. In other words, track the cost of your total opening inventory—your purchase cost and what you have left at year-end. At tax time, you will need to have an accurate total cost of what's sold to apply to your tax return.

Home Office

The home office can be a separate room or a portion of a room as long as you can adequately figure the square footage of the office from the rest of the house. (Inventory space, as long as it is attached to the house, such as in the basement, can be added onto the square footage of the office.) That separate office room or the percentage of the home office to the rest of the house will be applied to utilities, mortgage interest, property taxes, and home owner's insurance. Any repairs, and maintenance that directly affect that space, such as having work done to the heating system or the septic system is also deductible. If you purchase carpet, paint, furniture, and so on for that office specifically, those would be 100 percent usable for the business and would go on the same form. Figure 14-4 shows the form for expenses for business use of your home.

Figure 14-4   Form 8829 is the IRS form that pertains to expenses for business use of your home.

TIP: Tax accountant Lisa Jeck also states that, "A bona fide home office, according to the IRS, is an area of your home used regularly and exclusively for business purposes. A home office doesn't mean 40 hours a week, but that room or designated area must be used only for business."

Business Mileage

Whenever you travel from the home office, whether you go to the bank, the post office, a show, an estate sale, or 100 garage sales on a Saturday, you have deductible mileage. You need to keep track of your overall mileage for the whole year. If you don't have a separate business vehicle, you need to separate your business miles from your personal miles. For example, if out of your yearly mileage 20 percent was business, you have the option of (1) taking 20 percent of the operating cost and depreciating 20 percent of the car or (2) taking a cents per mile deduction (40.5 cents per mile presently). The cents per mile deduction includes repair, maintenace, upkeep, and insurance.

TIP: To keep track of business miles, buy a handy auto log mileage booklet at your local office supply store. Mileage can be a big deduction if you keep diligent records.

Purchase of Business Assets

The cost of business assets, such as a computer, digital camera, carpeting, shelving, and so on, is also a deductible expense. The IRS allows you to write off up to $100,000 of fixed assets each year for a small business. You're not obligated to that amount. You can depreciate the business assets (write them off over a series of years). Each type of asset has a number of years. For example, a computer has five years and furniture has seven years of depreciation. If you have a home office, you will have to depreciate part of your home in order to take this writeoff, and that is over 39 years, which is a miniscule portion.

TIP: The IRS has clarified how it treats the gain from the sale of your home. If you have a home office and you sell your home, the only amount you would have to declare is the depreciation you've written off over the years of having this business, which is a very small amount. If you have an outbuilding used as an office or a shop, the rules are different, and you would have to claim a gain or loss if you sold that entire property.

Telephone

A separate line in your house for business purposes is a deductible expense. However, if you don't have a separate business line, the IRS won't allow you to take a portion of your main phone line coming into the house. However, the IRS will allow you to deduct (in full) services such as RingMate, Call Waiting, and other specialty services that relate to your business.

TIP: Most everyone is mobile, and the IRS allows you to write off your cell phone if you use that cell phone for business purposes.

Credit Cards

Keep a separate credit card, if you use one, just for the business. The reason is that credit card interest that is personal is not deductible, but credit card interest for business purposes is deductible. Lisa Jeck says to remember that "it's the date you charge a purchase that creates a deduction, not the date you pay off the credit card. If you do not pay your card balances in full each month, you will be understating your deductions in the year of purchase and overstating them in the year the balance is paid."

Bank Accounts

If you operate as a sole proprietor, you can operate under your own Social Security Number. You don't need to have a tax identification number. But if you're operating under a business name that is not your own name, you have to go to the state and register that trade name. And if you bring the bank your trade name registration, you can open a business account under that business name. Usually you cannot deposit a check with a business name into a personal account. Make note that you are not required to keep a separate business account, but you can't deduct bank fees either.

Expense Caution

There are three areas of concern that you need to be careful of and to document. They are

- Meals
- Entertainment
- Travel

You want to make sure that the trip you do for business is predominantly for business. If you go away for a week, make sure that four or five of those days are for business. Travel is 100 percent deductible. But if you bring your spouse or children with you, unless they are part of the business, they won't qualify as a deduction for travel such as airfare. However, a motel room is acceptable. The IRS is not going to ask you to split the cost of the motel room.

With regard to meals, they are split in half (50 percent) on your tax return. If you do a show locally and you buy lunch, that is not a deductible expense for you, but if you take someone out to talk about business, that is deductible. For your benefit, keep track on the back of your receipt who you were with and why this is a deductible meal.

Again, entertainment is also 50 percent deductible. The IRS may check entertainment expenses, such as golf dates and sporting or theater tickets. Make sure that you are entertaining for business purposes and that you keep receipts as to whom you entertained and why.

TIP: Request a small business publication called "Publication 334" from the IRS. It is very informative for those just starting out.

Partnership

If you're in a partnership, according to the IRS, you have a separate entity that would file its own tax return. That tax return does not have taxes paid on it. It's a reporting document to state here's what the business made or lost. From that, schedules are given out to each of the partners to prepare their own taxes. With a partnership, return taxation is treated like a sole proprietorship.

ETHICS

In this business, you may hear stories or come across situations that raise some ethical questions. First, I would like to discuss a few categories that, as a beginner, you may want to avoid. And then I will discuss three cases that are relevant to this business (one case is in litigation).

With regard to certain items, use your best judgment as to whether or not you want to sell controversial merchandise. There are other categories, but these three come to mind because I've dealt directly with all three. These items are

- Weapons
- Furs
- Nazi memorabilia

We are a much more aware and cautious society since 9/11. And even though some of the weapons may be old and valuable, you need to ask yourself, "Do I want to sell something that potentially may hurt someone else?"

Many states have laws about gun and antique firearms. Permits are needed, and paperwork must be filed with the state. eBay doesn't allow the selling of firearms. Please consult an expert in this area if you are interested in firearms. Other weapons such as knives are very collectible and can be sold on eBay. From an ethical standpoint, try to make sure that you are selling to an adult collector.

Many people are against the buying and selling of authentic fur coats or lifelike "stuffed" animal skins. You have to ask yourself, "Is it okay for me? And what about my clientele? Or are animal pelts and furs better for someone else to handle?"

The other area of concern is Nazi memorabilia. eBay prohibits it, although you can sell certain German war memorabilia. Many auction companies won't accept Nazi material to sell at their auctions. Most of this memorabilia is sold privately to collectors. Ask at different shops to see if the shop owners know anyone who collects this type of merchandise. And again, you have to be the judge as to whether or not you want to buy and sell this kind of memorabilia. Owing to the recent escapades of Prince Harry who wore a Nazi uniform to a party, the European countries are considering banning the sale of all Nazi-related items.

The following stories are brought to your attention not so much for the story itself but for the ethical questions that arise as a result of these purchases. Please note that the stories may have strayed somewhat from the truth, but the principles for each case are the same. Some day you could find yourself in a similar situation. And what would you do if this happened to you?

It's Only a Game

As the story goes, a man went to a yard sale and purchased a board game for $2. The man opened the game to see if all the pieces were inside. Lo and behold, the game had real money inside—over $10,000. The woman claimed the game wasn't supposed to be sold. The case went to court. The court ruled in favor of the man who purchased the game, claiming that the rule of "finders keepers" applied. Do you agree with the court's ruling? Would you return the money to the seller? Or split the money with the seller? What if you were the seller in this case? How would you feel?

Mother and Child Reunion

This case drew national media attention and happened only 30 minutes from where I live. The story goes that three friends pooled their money and purchased an old painting of the Madonna and Child for $3,200 at a church auction in Dublin, New Hampshire. They took the painting to Sotheby's auction in New York City. The experts dated the painting to the fourteenth century and concluded that it was the missing third panel of a triptych. The painting sold at auction for a little under half a million dollars ($489,600). Here are some questions to think about:

- Should the trio share any of their profits with the church? Would you?
- Should the trio share their profits with the local woman that donated the painting (and received no money) in the first place? Would you?

Pooling is when two or more parties decide not to bid against each other so that they can purchase something at a lower price. According to auction law, pooling is illegal, but the law is rarely enforced because it is so hard to prove. In this case, will the church try to prove pooling? Would you?

He's Not a Poker Face

Jim Houghton, of White Wolf Antiques, went to a yard sale in a very poor neighborhood. He bought some poker chips in a container for $1 from a woman who really needed the money. It turned out that the poker chips were Bakelite (a very collectible form of plastic). He listed the poker chips on eBay, where they sold for $500. End of story, right? Would that be the end of the story if you had purchased those poker chips? Jim felt so bad for the woman that he returned to the woman's house and gave her half the money from the sale of the poker chips. The woman wept because she didn't have enough money to pay her rent until Jim split the profits with her.

Passion, honesty, and integrity are precursors to maintaining a successful business and your reputation. Do you like to talk, meet a variety of people, and sell anything from A to Z? Become an auctioneer or an antique dealer or both. Do you want to set your own hours, correspond with people all over the world, and still relax in the comfort of your own home? Become an eBay specialist.

Think of a good business name, pay your taxes, have fun, be passionate, and go out there and make a living. Your fortune is waiting just around the corner—at the next estate sale, garage sale, auction, or flea market. Quick! Go find your treasure. I've given you all the secrets to success. Now go out there and "Do it!" And for more inspiration to get you fired up, read the next chapter on success stories and insider tips from others who have made their fortune.

15

"Eureka! I Found It!" Success Stories from Those Who Found a Treasure

---

Eureka actually originates from the California Gold Rush days. When searchers for gold came across a vein of gold, they would shout, "Eureka!" meaning "I found it." This chapter is meant to capture those high moments of buying and selling when someone, either a novice or an experienced pro, has "found it," meaning that they found that treasure, that fortune, that tip, or that idea that satisfied them or kept them searching for more.

The following tips and stories are from people who willingly shared their experiences about finding their greatest fortune in hopes that you, too, will make your fortune. For easy reading, the chapter is divided into these sections:

- General buying—auctions, eBay, and garage sales
- General selling—auctions, eBay, flea markets/shows, and shops
- Treasure stories—a few examples of great finds and their results

TIPS ON BUYING

A consensus in the business is to "buy what you know." And then there are some people who say, "Buy what you don't know." When it comes down to it, you have to decide what is comfortable for you and your budget.

Buying in General

Don't buy something just to buy it. Listen to your gut, watch what others are buying, surf eBay to see what's selling, spend the day at a museum to look at quality antiques, or read a price guide or reference book. Following are some general guidelines that people shared with me:

"You make your money when you buy, not when you sell; you just don't know how much. If you pay too much, you can't turn it over. If you pay short, you can sell it whenever you want."—Guy Trudel, Sr., auctioneer and owner, Trudel's Auction Gallery, Bellingham, Massachusetts

"You can never pay too much for anything you collect, only too soon." —Bob Taylor, antique dealer for 30 years, Warwick, Rhode Island

"Don't buy. Get a current price guide and go out and look first."—John G., Coca-Cola collector, Coon Rapids, Minnesota

"It's a gamble. It's a crapshoot. But at least you know you're going to get something back for your money."—Bob Stefanik, S & J Antiques, Seekonk, Massachusetts

TIP: Watch out for goods that you may suddenly acquire from a suspicious source. They may be stolen. The best solution is to call the police and report the incident so that you aren't the one being accused.

"Take your date to an auction or a flea market. If you both get hooked on antiques, who knows what you will buy or where that can lead."— Phyllis Lodder, East Brookfield, Massachusetts

"Don't impulse buy. That's a big mistake."—William Lodder, East Brookfield, Massachusetts

"Buy what you love, and then, if you get stuck with it, at least you can live with it."—Barbara Lee-Roberts, 20-year veteran in the business, Peterborough, New Hampshire

"If you buy and sell what you like, you'll go broke. You have to buy what sells."—Terry Zahuranec, T+room Antiques, Horscheads, New York

"Pick something there isn't a book on and buy it. Go to school. People go to school to be doctors and lawyers. Experience is the world's greatest teacher. Specific fields merit specific knowledge and specific knowledge begets money."—Toby Castle, The One Man Band, Kimball, Minnesota

"Go around and learn about items. See what other pieces are selling for. Pick one or two items and learn about them. You've got to have knowledge in this business."—Joe Allard, Connecticut antique dealer for 45 years

"There is plenty of the common stuff to go around, so if you buy, buy condition. The better the condition, the better the investment."— David Capizzano, antique tool collector, Westerly, Rhode Island

"If you're a beginner, don't pay a lot because you won't get hurt for paying too much."—Steve Gass, garage sale and auction "junkie," Norwich, Connecticut

"You don't learn anything from your hits; you learn from your mistakes. You bought something for $25 and you had to sell it for $5. You got a $20 education. You pay for your education. You'll never make that mistake again and that was a cheap education."—Helen Louth, owner of The Hope Chest, Johnston, Rhode Island

"Buy jewelry; it's easy to carry, pack, and ship."—Ginger Castle, graduate gemologist, Minneapolis, Minnesota

"Don't let anyone tell you what to buy and what not to buy. Go with your gut. Buy the unusual, something you haven't seen before or something that is ugly."—Bob Glass, Sr., Hall of Fame Auctioneer, Estero, Florida

Buying at Auctions

Although Chapter 12 mentions various tips on buying at auction, here are a few more for you to consider:

"Buy storage units that come up for auction. You have to take the good with the bad. Just remember, most of the good stuff is buried in the bottom."—Thory Heye, owner, Heritage Auctions, Clinton, Connecticut

"Buy something that the auctioneer didn't advertise."—Bob Stefanik, S & J Antiques, Seekonk, Massachusetts

TIP: At an auction, if you see items around the yard used as landscaping and you're interested in these things, ask to have them put up for sale near the end of the auction. You can get a better deal on them when the crowd has thinned out.

"Never buy anything you haven't looked at physically during inspection. If something is going for a bargain at auction, and you wonder why, don't be tempted to bid unless you can look the item over to make sure it isn't damaged."—Scott Downer, Connecticut antique dealer

"The customer who is not a dealer always says, 'I can't buy anything because the dealers pay too much,' meaning the dealer knows the value of the item. If a customer can buy that item one bid above the dealer, she got a good buy. Why? If that customer goes to the dealer's shop, he or she is going to pay 50 percent higher anyway."—Bob Ward, Auctioneer, Ashaway, Rhode Island

"Go early to an auction and inspect the items carefully. Have an idea of what you want to pay. Too many people get carried away and over-bid. It's an ego thing. Know what you're bidding on."—Phil Liver-ant, antique dealer for 50 years, Colchester, Connecticut

Doug Matteson, a long-time furniture dealer from North Kingstown, Rhode Island, suggests the following:

- Look for good quality and good condition in used furniture. You don't have to know a lot about furniture that you like. If you like it, someone else will.
- Buy the first or second item of the auction because no one is ready, and the crowd isn't used to the auctioneer yet.
- Buy something right after a big-ticket item (meaning something that sold for a lot of money). People are in awe about the price and haven't recovered from that yet.
- Go to sheriff's auctions—usually it's an eviction of some kind, and a lot of unadvertised things go up for bid. (These sales are advertised in the classified sections of the newspaper.)

Buying on eBay

Millions of items are up for bid on eBay every week. It's easy to register and bid. Look for sellers with little experience and sellers who don't know how to describe something they have. You can be notified via e-mail when certain items that you're looking for are listed on eBay. You can get some good deals. Here are some of them:

"Look for new eBayers, those sellers who have 100 sales or under; 0 to 10 is even better. Look for words that are misspelled because the seller may not know what he has."—John G., Coon Rapids, Minnesota

"Look for sellers that have lots of feedback. See how long they've been selling. Get a feel for how they write. E-mail questions to the seller."—Barbara van der Lyke, williams712, eBay PowerSeller

Muffie Calabrese, longtime antique dealer and eBay buyer and seller (muffstuff) offers these four tips for buying on eBay:

1. "Take advantage of Auction Sniper if you really want something. It makes buying less frustrating and you don't have to sit in front of the computer to keep placing your bid.

2. I never bid an even number; I always add cents on to my last bid. The number that works best for me is $25.37. Don't round the number off to $25.25. People tend to do that or bid in 50-cent increments and then they are never successful.

3. Items tend to look bigger in the pictures than they are in reality and you can be disappointed if the vase is a miniature. Always e-mail the seller about measurements.

4. Don't forget about the postage when you are bidding and ask for a shipping rate ahead of time. Some sellers are not fair when it comes to shipping charges. I stay away from them."

Buying at Garage and Other Sales

Remember that the key is to go early and be the first one at the sale. You will find more treasures this way. Plot out your treasure map as described in Chapter 3, and try to single out unadvertised sales for the best buys.

"Buy what you don't know. You're not going to lose much if you buy something for $10 and under. I bought something for $2 and had no idea what it was. I took it to an expert at Skinner's in Bolton, Massachusetts. They identified it as a sewing tool for sails on ships, and it sold at auction for $650."—David Ledversis, antique dealer from Rhode Island

"Look for sales that advertise dinettes and dryers. Chances are they are cleaning out the entire house. Go to the wealthier streets first. Don't be in a hurry to rush off to the next sale, if the people are still setting up their sale. If you sense there are older items up for sale, just hang out for a minute and make a second pass at items."—Tom Knoblauch, tac2000, eBay PowerSeller

"If a yard sale is advertised as a moving sale, and you have time, drive by the night before to see if a 'For Sale' sign is out front, then you know it should be a good sale."—Steve Gass, Norwich, Connecticut

"Go to the yard sale, the day before it is scheduled to open, to see if you can buy anything prior to the sale. That's when you'll find the best items."—Peggy Russ, Quaker Hill, Connecticut.

"The most important thing to look for in a garage sale ad is the time of the sale. If the sale says 8–1 or 9–12, I know these folks have had a sale before. I look for sales that end at 4 or 5 in the afternoon. These people have probably never had a garage sale before; therefore, the pickings and the prices will be better."—Tom Knoblauch, tac2000, eBay PowerSeller

TIP: Go to yard sales that are two to five miles down an old country road, because no one else will.

TIPS ON SELLING

Just as there are many places to buy, there are as many markets in which to sell your goods. Experiment and see what works for you. And read here what works for others.

Selling in General

"Look at it for what it isn't rather than what it is (and then sell it)."—Robert Taylor, antique dealer, Warwick, Rhode Island

"Find something that you can salvage like old typewriter keys [see Figure 15-1] and make them into something functional. We take old typewriter keys and make them into sterling silver monogrammed jewelry."—Ray and Rhonda Barske, co-owners of Typewriterjewelry.com

Figure 15-1   Old typewriter keys like these are rescued from defunct typewriters and turned into beautiful monogrammed jewelry.

"Before the days of eBay, I sold at flea markets for a fast turnover of goods; co-ops for better antiques; and auctions for prime items."—Barbara Lee-Roberts, owner of Spice...s Nice

"Half of selling is to learn your product, ask questions and read. I got started in the business because I bought a tin of buttons and sorted them. In the beginning, I didn't know what I had. Now I know more and belong to the National Button Association. Learn your product because you can talk about it."—Kristine Tibbetts, Florida

Selling at Auction

A profitable place to sell is the auction market, whether you consign to a local auctioneer or to a high-end gallery in the city. You also may want to try your hand as an auctioneer one day.

"Get to know your auctioneer. Does he own it? Is he the agent only? Does the estate have the right to bid? Are the items sold with or without reserve?"—Robert Glass, Sr., Hall of Fame Auctioneer, Estero, Florida

"If a client has enough similar items or a house full of merchandise, or finds that they have to liquidate an estate, they should have an on-site auction. That's the best way of obtaining the most money in the shortest amount of time."—Robert Glass, Jr., auctioneer and appraiser, Sterling, Connecticut

"I always tell the client don't complain about the price for each item. Some items go high, and some go low. You have to look at the bottom line, the overall gross of the auction. And then they are usually happy."—Bob Ward, auctioneer, Ashaway, Rhode Island

"Working in the auction business beats punching a clock and working 9 to 5, although in reality you work many more hours because it's your own business."—Guy Trudel, Sr., Trudel's Auction Gallery, Bellingham, Massachusetts

Selling on eBay

Millions of people are selling their treasures on eBay. Here are a few more good reasons to sell on eBay:

"You get 40 to 50 people looking at that one specific item; you wouldn't get 40 or 50 people to come into your shop to look at that one item. For us, selling on eBay is good all year, except right around income tax time."—Barbara van der Lyke, williams712, eBay PowerSeller

"The Internet has brought the world closer. Prices for common things have dropped. You now have more high-end collectors and more competition for the better pieces."—Ellen Rubell, "The Wedgwood Lady," Wallingford, Connecticut

"A different age group is collecting today and they buy according to how old they are, not how old the items are. They like things from the 1950s and 1960s, so I make sure I list items that I think will sell."—Muffie Calabrese, antique dealer and eBay seller (muffstuff).

Tom Knoblauch, tac2000, eBay PowerSeller, says that 95 percent of his eBay items come from garage sales. He tries to find old items or newer items that seem like good quality. Tom offers these general eBay tips:
- Put on things that you don't care about, and you will never be disappointed with the final bid.
- Start your item well below its value, and do not put a reserve on it. You will have many early bids this way. When people are outbid, they tend to come back, and all the bids will create an interest in your item that will get more people looking.
- Don't be greedy. If you see that an item just like yours closed for $100 the week before, don't start your item at $100 or even $75. Start the item much lower, such as $5 or $10. If you're following the first rule, this is no problem.
- Prime time. Always make sure that your sale ends between 8 and 12 P.M. Eastern Standard Time Sunday through Thursday. This is when most people are on eBay, and it's your best chance for a big snipe or an impulse buyer. Never end your item on a Saturday afternoon or other slow time.
- Buy your stuff cheap. Unless you know for sure what you're buying, don't spend too much for your stuff. Make it up with quantity of items.

Selling Out of Your Shop

Many dealers prefer to have their own shop for various reasons. They like to own their own business, work out of their own house, set their own hours, and converse with customers. Here are a few more helpful hints:

"You have to put other things in the window besides the high-end stuff; otherwise the customer won't go into that 'museum' shop. Keep your hours and return phone calls. If you don't return the phone calls, they will call someone else."—Una Smith, owner of Granite Hill Antiques, Westerly, Rhode Island

"I've always been in the high rent district. It's important not to take what I can't sell. If you want to be the best of the best, you have to take the best of the best. When people see high volume, they think high profit, and that equates to a customer, you must be a million-aire, but I make my living on the last 8 cents. So it's really important to be the best."—Helen Louth, owner of The Hope Chest, Johnston, Rhode Island

"Four important aspects come to mind if you want to own your own shop: (1) Location, Location, Location! (2) Get guidance from an expert in small business development. (3) Keep on top of what is selling. (4) Use the Internet. I love books, but if you don't understand the business side, you'll be in trouble. Contact a local university and find a management counselor in the business department. Often they offer advice and planning for small businesses. We've saved a tremendous amount of money and have been able to expand our business by using their guidelines. We've been in business for 35 years, and because of the Internet, our business has grown. For a standard monthly fee, we are registered to sell online at www.abebooks.com. This service lists online bookstores that carry our books. More than 25 percent of our business now comes from the Internet."—Vicky Uminowicz, Titcomb's Bookshop on Cape Cod, East Sandwich, Massachusetts

"My daughter started out with a degree at the Fashion Institute of Technology in New York. She's always been interested in vintage clothing. I advised her to open a shop. We came up with a name for the shop because I don't like goodbye's and always told my family to say, 'So long, never say goodbye.' Now, six years later, we have two shops that are filled with more than just vintage clothing—one on the Vineyard and one in Connecticut."—Isabelle Russo, Never Say Goodbye Antiques, Oak Bluffs, Massachusetts

Selling at Flea Markets and Shows

Flea markets and shows are a fun and profitable way to sell your treasures. Make sure that you are equipped with merchandise, supplies, and help so that you last through the day. Here are a few more tips:

"To increase your profits, get a man to stop at your table. Get them to take their hands out of their pockets. Have crossbows, knives, and lighters so they will stop, look, and touch. Make sure the men are occupied so the women have a longer time to look and buy."—Barbara Lee-Roberts, owner of Spice . . .s Nice, Peterborough, New Hampshire

"Have a good atmosphere. Don't be sarcastic. Be a great salesperson and have a sense of humor to make people feel comfortable. Make them feel good about what they are buying so they will return."
—Jeff Izzo, antique dealer, Plainfield, Connecticut

"You make your money on opening day at any show, and you make it before it's open to the public."—Dick and Jan Kekelik, antique dealers for 18 years at New England Motel, Brimfield Shows, Brimfield, Massachusetts

"Educate yourself. If your merchandise isn't selling, watch what is being carried out."—Terry Zahuranec, T+ room Antiques, New York

"Mark your tags bold and large with the price. If the price is small, it shows you're not sure about your price."—Barbara Lee-Roberts, owner of Spice . . .s Nice, Peterborough, New Hampshire

"Don't clutter your booth. Let it have an open, inviting look. Make it wheel chair accessible. Don't sit in the booth. Sit on the edges, out of the way."—Ed Correia, owner of Under the Pine Antiques and Collectibles, Sterling, Connecticut

TIP: Sell something that you can wear and others can wear." Kristine Tibbetts, "The Button Lady," makes her own button bracelets, wears them at shows, and sells them. See Figure 15-2.

Figure 15-2   Inventive button bracelet with popular Scottie Dog button sells for $35.

"Don't ignore your customer. Don't sit there and read a book. Greet them. Silence is silence. Say something to them. It will put money in your pocket."—Kristine Tibbetts, "The Button Lady"

STORIES TO TREASURE

This section is about people who have found a piece of "junk" that became a treasure because of what they did with that piece once it was theirs. From reading these stories, you may decide that you will want to try "dumpster diving" or stop at those thrift stores instead of driving by them. Or maybe you'll research a piece of glassware or focus on one particular specialty market, such as cameras or violins. I have included a few stories that are meant to give you inspiration to buy or sell. Whether it's an auction, a garage sale, a flea market, or a show, you can find that treasure too.

Free TV

Jeff G. goes "dumpster diving" regularly. He lives in a condo complex and checks the dumpsters every Sunday night and at the end of the month, when people usually move. Among other salable items, Jeff's best find was a floor model big screen TV that had nothing wrong with it. He sold it for $300 at an auction.

A Wrenching Story

David Capizzano has been an avid antique carpenter tool collector for 30 years. He bought a wrench for $80 at an auction in Connecticut and sold it to a tool dealer in New York for $1,150. At that time, it was a record price for a wrench.

Car Care

Tom Knoblauch went to a sale at 7:00 A.M. for a 9:00 A.M. start. No one opened the door. He was about to leave when he noticed that the license plate on the Cadillac in the driveway read, "VETERN." This little fact made Tom go back and knock again because the caddy was older than a Vietnam-era car. Tom bought $30 worth of stuff from an old guy. From that sale, he sold a Hot Wheel car for $535 and a daguerreotype for $1,165.

Lamp Light

Steve bought a millefiori glass lamp at a yard sale for $5. From his research, he dated the lamp to 1910 and sold it on eBay for $1,200. Millefiori is a multicolored intricate glass pattern that consists of cut glass canes.

Music to My Ears

While he was on a business trip, John bought a saxophone for $300 at a pawnshop. The saxophone was a Conn with a detailed engraving of a naked lady (signifying vintage 1920s). John sold the saxophone on eBay for $1,300.

Give That Man a Cigar

Clark van der Lyke bought what looked like a large wooden cigar box for $3 at a local yard sale. It was in fair condition. He repaired and cleaned it and took it to city hall to give to his city manager, who smokes cigars. The city manager rejected the box because it wasn't a humidor (a tight-fitting box to keep his cigars fresh). So Clark kept the box in his office and used it for pencils. Then when he tired of it, he took it home and listed it on eBay. A dealer from Nantucket bought the box for $1,500. It turned out that the box was an early seamen's sewing or "ditty" box with whalebone and ivory decorations.

"It's the Real Thing."

John Glass bought a metal, full-size policeman who advertised, "Drink Coca-Cola" on the reverse side with an iron base that was also inscribed "Coca-Cola." In the 1950s, a policeman statue, like this one, was placed at school crossings. John bought the sign for $100, and it is valued today at $1,500. One in mint condition would bring about $1,800. See Figure 15-3. For John, this find is a treasure and adds to the value of his extensive Coca-Cola collection.

Tupperware Party

John Dinsdale of Fox Hill Antiques, Pomfret, CT drove by a "Tupperware and Toy" yard sale and almost didn't stop. But gut instinct and 40 years of antique experience told him to go back. His treasure was in the table that was under all the plastic goods. John bought the Gustav Stickley table for $15 and later sold it to a private collector for $3,000.

Good Will

Deborah Jurczyk, a Connecticut and Rhode Island antique dealer, bought a pair of 1950s chairs at a Goodwill Store for $30. She sold them at a show to a Long Island, New York, dealer for $350. He reupholstered them and sold them to a customer for $3,500. She was happy with what she made, and so was the New York dealer and the customer who ended up with the chairs.

TIP: "When you visit pawnshops, thrift stores, or consignment shops, ask the owner if they have anything else in the back that they haven't put out on the floor yet. If you are very specific, you may find your fortune."—Connie Caswell, Boston, Massachusetts

Figure 15-3   This 1950s Coca-Cola policeman advertisement is worth $1,500. *(Photo courtesy of John Glass.)*

Smile for the Camera

James Hutchinson, eclectic collector from Tolland, Connecticut, bought a vintage camera in bric-a-brac shop in New York for $40. The item had been in the shop less than an hour. The camera was a Leica M3 Canadian single reflex lens camera. He sold the camera at a collector's meet for $4,000.

Your Autograph Please

Robert H. Glass bought an old *Life Magazine* for $1 at a garage sale. The cover had a picture of Paul Newman on it. Robert asked Paul Newman to sign it, and the *Life Magazine* sold for $4,500. The money was donated to Paul Newman's Hole in the Wall Gang Camp auction for kids with cancer and blood-related diseases.

A Nice Mug Shot

Kim May, an eBay PowerSeller whose user ID is Kimamay, bought a damaged one-quart pewter tankard from a clearance rack at an antique show for $5 (see Figure 15-4). Kim almost didn't buy the piece because it was so dented and cracked. She listed the tankard on eBay, and it sold for $3,050 to a collector in Massachusetts. It turns out that the tankard is a rare seventeenth-century American-made piece. Only three are known to exist.

The Lucky Buddha

Robert Glass, Jr., auctioneer and appraiser, first became hooked on yard sales in high school. Bob went to a church yard sale and found an oriental Buddha that looked like one he saw in his history book. The Buddha was marked $5. Instead of using that money for his lunch, he bought the statue. On recommendation from his father, he took the Buddha to Christie's Auction House, where it sold for $5,000. With that money, Bob took his entire history class to lunch.

Cuckoo Clock Timing

Barbara R. collected cuckoo clocks for many years. She picked them up at garage sales and flea markets for $5 and $10 and hung them up in her house. They were all in working order and chimed every half hour. When her husband died suddenly, she sold the collection at auction (at least $5,000) to pay the mortgage through the winter.

Figure 15-4 Seventeenth-century pewter tankard purchased for $5 from a clearance rack at an antique show sold for $3050 on eBay. *(Photo courtesy of Kim May.)*

Fit for a King or Queen

Helen Louth, owner of The Hope Chest in Johnston, Rhode Island, had a woman bring a scepter into her consignment shop. The woman bought the scepter in Washington. She had all the documentation (provenance) for it. Helen and the owner of the scepter decided to mark it $150. It didn't sell. Six months later, the woman brought it back. This time it sold for $95 on the last markdown to a dealer in Newport. He sold it to a gentleman who put the scepter into an auction at Christie's in New York. The scepter sold for $10,000.

Record Player/Record Price

Fred Ford, of Fred's New England Antiques, in North Kingstown, Rhode Island, bought an old upright Victor Victrola at auction for $400. He put it in his shop for $620. Nobody was interested. He put it up on eBay and got an offer of $4,000 to sell it early and take it off the eBay auction. Fred decided to leave it on eBay for the seven days. The Victrola sold for $6,000 to a collector in Indiana who drove out to Connecticut to pick up the Victrola personally. It was a rare early custom-made Victrola of which very few were made.

No Fiddling Around

Connie Caswell is a fiddler. She is passionate about playing, and she is always looking for violins. One day an inner voice told her to call a certain thrift store. After a while, she did, and she asked the owner if he had any violins. He had three. She asked him to hold the violins until she got off work. Connie bought all three of them for a total of only $125. She knew one was a treasure. She took the violin to a world-renowned violin expert in Boston, who identified the violin as a Paul Bailly violin worth $10,000 to $15,000. See Figure 15-5. Although Connie has fallen in love with this violin (a more common occurrence than not), she still feels that she has a treasure, no matter how much money it is worth, because of the beautiful sounds the violin produces when she plays it.

TIP: Did you know that stolen violins have wanted posters with "mug shots"? Many fake violins with fake labels and signatures are on the market. Make sure that you know what you are buying and that the item is not stolen property.

Duck, Duck, Goose

Loys Gubernick from Lynnfield, Massachusetts, bought a damaged gray shorebird in an antique store in Connecticut for $15 because she liked it. A

Figure 15-5   Paul Bailly violin bought in a thrift store for $50 is appraised for over $10,000. *(Photo courtesy of B. D. Colen/ADIOL.)*

friend of hers found out that it was valuable because of the maker, Elmer Crowell. She consigned the painted shorebird to a New York gallery, and it sold at auction for $12,800. With the proceeds from the sale of the bird, she took her entire family on a cruise.

So this brings us to the end of this book but not to the end of the story. I would like to hear your story. Please e-mail me at trashtotreasure @mac.com. I'd love to hear about your tips and treasure finds. Remember, your fortune is waiting—at the next garage sale, auction, flea market, or show or on eBay. So go out there and find it! Good luck and happy treasure hunting.

Resources

Atlantique City
Atlantic City Convention Center
(800) 526-2724
www.atlantiquecity.com
Largest indoors antique and collectible show, held in October

Brimfield Antique and Collectible Show
Along Route 20, Brimfield, MA
Outdoor show, held three times a year – May, July, and September
Twenty different privately owned and operated shows with over 5,000 dealers
New England Motel site: www.antiques-brimfield.com

Ellis Antiques Show
Boston, MA
(617) 248-8571
www.ellisantiques.com
In November at the Boston Park Plaza Hotel, forty-fifth year

New York Armory Antique Show
67th and Park Avenue
New York City
www.winterantiquesshow.com

San Francisco Fall Antiques Show
200 Pine Street, Suite 600
San Francisco, CA 94105
(415) 989-9019
www.sffas.org
Oldest show on the West Coast
In October at Fort Mason Center

Every major city or state fairground may have an annual, semiannual, or quarterly antique show. Do a search on the Web in the state in which you're interested.

AUCTIONS

Alderfer Auction Company
501 Fairground Road
Hatfield, PA 19440
(215) 393-3000
www.alderferauction.com

Bonham's & Butterfields
7601 Sunset Boulevard
Los Angeles, CA 90046
(800) 223-2854
www.bonhams.com/us

Christie's
20 Rockefeller Plaza
New York, NY 10020
(212) 636-2000
www.christies.com

Dixon's Furniture Auction
Route 544 and Route 290
Crumpton, MD
(410) 928-3006
Huge weekly (Wednesday) outdoor and indoor year-round auction event

Garth's Auctions, Inc.
2690 Stratford Road
Delaware, OH 43015
(740) 362-4771
www.garths.com
Early American antiques and decorative arts

James D. Julia, Inc.
P.O. Box 830
Fairfield, ME 04937
(207) 453-7125
www.juliaauctions.com
Firearms, lamps, glass, toys, and dolls

Skinner's, Inc.
63 Park Plaza
Boston, MA 02116
(617) 350-5400
Bolton, MA

(978) 779-6241
www.skinnerinc.com
Appraisers and auctioneers of fine art and antiques

Sotheby's
72nd and York Streets
New York, NY
(888) 752-0002
www.sothebys.com

A directory of auctioneers is often in your local newspaper, or go to the National Association for a state-by-state membership guide at www.auctioneers.org.

BOOKS, DIRECTORIES, AND GUIDES

Collectible Price Guide, by Judith Miller (New York: DK Publishing, Inc). Yearly price guide.

Gale Directory of Publications and Broadcast Media, 5 vols., by Gale Group, Inc., 27500 Drake Road, Farmington Hills, MI 48331, www.gale.com. Annual guide to international publications and broadcasting systems.

Garage Sale & Flea Market Annual, by Bob and Sharon Huxford (Kentucky: Collector Books). Yearly price guide.

Guide to Best Flea Markets in 50 States, by Albert Lafarge (St. Martin's Press, May 2000)

Hammered Aluminum: Hand Wrought Collectibles, by Dannie A. Woodard and Billie J. Wood, 1983, and Book II, 1993.

How to Sell Anything on eBay and Make a Fortune, by Dennis L. Prince (New York: McGraw-Hill, 2004).

Kovels' Antiques & Collectibles Price List, by Ralph and Terry Kovel (New York: Random House). Yearly price guide.

New England Newspaper Directory, by New England Press Association, 360 Huntington Avenue 428CP, Boston, MA 02115. (617) 373-5610. Directory of advertising rates and data.

Official Directory to U.S. Flea Markets, by Kitty Werner (New York: Random House, May 2002)

Official Guide to Flea Market Prices, by Harry L. Rinker (New York: Random House, 2003)

Schroeder's Antiques Price Guide, edited by Bob and Sharon Huxford (Kentucky: Schroeder Publishing Co.). Yearly guide.

The Pocket Idiot's Guide to Garage and Yard Sales, by Cathy Pedigo and Sonia Weiss (New York: Alpha Books, 2003)

The Standard Periodical Directory. Oxbridge Communications, 186 Fifth Avenue, Sixth Floor, New York, NY 10010. (212) 741-0231. www.mediafinder.com. Nationwide directory

Wanted to Buy: A Listing of Serious Buyers Paying Cash for Everything Collectible! 7th ed., by Bob and Sharon Huxford (Kentucky: Collector Books, 1999)

Warman's Antiques and Collectibles Price Guides, edited by Ellen T. Schroy (Wisconsin: Krause Publications). Yearly.

Specialized guides are available on any topic, such as Avon, Barbies, bottles, Civil War, comics, Fisher-Price, golf, jewelry, knives, movies, Native American, political, quilts, records, stamps, textiles, watches. Check your local or online bookstore.

FLEA MARKETS

Long Beach Outdoor Antique and Collectible Market
Lakewood Blvd. and Conant Street
Long Beach, CA
(323) 655-5703
Operates third Sunday of every month
Named as one of the top 10 flea markets by *Good Housekeeping*

Renninger's
740 Noble Street
Kutztown, PA
www.renningers.com
Open weekly with three special antique shows
Over 1,200 dealers from 42 states
Antique extravaganza shows April, June, and September
Phone M–F: (877) 385-0104

Renningers
Route 117
MT. Dora, FL
www.renningers.com
Open every weekend
Antique extravaganza third weekend of January, February, and November
Antique center, farmer and flea markets
(352) 383-8393

Shipshewana Auction and Flea Market
345 S. Van Buren Street
P.O. Box 185
Shipshewana, IN 46565
(260) 768-4129
May–October
Tuesdays and Wednesdays
1,000 flea market vendors
Also hold auctions

Traders Village Flea Market
Eldridge Road
Houston, TX 77083
(281) 890-5500
800 dealers on 60 acres
Open Saturday & Sunday from 9–6, 12 months a year

Check the flea market directories above for a more complete listing of flea markets
  across the country.

MAGAZINES/JOURNALS

Art & Antiques
P.O. Box 660
MT Morris, IL 61054
(815) 734-1162
www.artandantiques.net
Covers trends across the country

Country Home
P.O. Box 37244
Boone, IA 50037
(800) 374-9431
www.countryhome.com

Country Living
P.O. Box 7138
Red Oak, IA 51591
(800) 888-0128
www.countryliving.com

Family Circle
375 Lexington Avenue
New York, NY 10017
(800) 627-4444
www.familycircle.com

House Beautiful
P.O. Box 7024
Red Oak, IA 51591
(515) 282-1508
www.housebeautful.com

Martha Stewart Living
11 West 42nd Street
New York, NY 10036
(212) 827-8000
www.marthastewart.com

New England Antiques Journal
24 Water Street
Palmer, MA 01609
(800) 432-3505
www.antiquesjournal.com
Monthly journal about auctions and shows; feature stories

Southeastern Antiquing and Collecting Magazine
P.O. Box 510
Acworth, GA 30101
(888) 388-7827
www.go-star.com/antiquing

The Antiquer
P.O. Box 2054
New York, NY 10159
(888) 294-9750
www.theantiquer.net
Comprehensive fine art and antiques monthly

The Magazine Antiques
575 Broadway
New York, NY 10012
(212) 941-2800
www.themagazineantiques.com
Art and antique monthly about the latest trends in fine and decorative arts

Woman's Day
1633 Broadway
New York, NY 10019
(212) 767-6000
www.womansday.com

Yankee Magazine
P.O. Box 520
Dublin, NH 03444
(603) 563-8111
www.yankeemagazine.com
Published 10 times a year; New England articles

You may have other favorite magazines or journals that talk about trends, flea markets, antiques, and auctions.

NEWSPAPERS

Antique Trader Weekly
2728 Asbury Road
P.O. Box 1050
Dubuque, IA 52004
(563) 588-2073
www.antiquetrader.com
Weekly newspaper about antiques and collectibles

AntiqueWeek
27 North Jefferson Street

P.O. Box 90
Knightstown, IN 46148
(800) 876-5133
www.antiqueweek.com
Regional and national auction information

Antiques & Auction News
P.O. Box 500
Mount Joy, PA 17552
(800) 800-1833
www.antiquesandauctionnews.net
Published weekly by Joel Sater

Antiques and the Arts Weekly—"The Bee"
5 Church Hill Road
P.O. Box 5503
Newtown, CT 06470
(203) 426-3141
www.AntiquesandTheArts.com
Weekly newspaper with shows, auctions, and articles of interest

Maine Antique Digest (M.A.D.)
P.O. Box 1429
Waldoboro, ME 04572
(800) 752-8521
www.maineantiquedigest.com
Worldwide marketplace for Americana, published monthly

Northeast Journal
388 Main Street
Catskill, NY 12414
(518) 943-5220
www.northeastjournal.com
Monthly publication about antiques, art, interior design

The New York Antique Almanac
P.O. Box 2400
New York, NY 10021
(212) 988-2700
Bimonthly publication of art and antiques

The WANT ADvertiser
128 Boston Post Road
Sudbury, MA 01776
(978) 443-7007
www.thewantad.com
Lists items for sale or swap

Published every Tuesday
Serving New England

Treasure Chest
P.O. Box 1120
Attleboro, MA 02703
(508) 236-0378
www.tcantiques.com
Information for collectors and dealers

Uncle Henry's Weekly Swap or Sell It Guide
525 Eastern Avenue
P.O. Box 9104
Augusta, ME 04230
(207) 623-1411
www.unclehenrys.com
Lists items for sale or swap
Published every Thursday
Serving New England and New Brunswick, Canada

UNRAVEL the GAVEL
14 Hurricane Road, No. 201
Belmont, NH 03220
(603) 524-4281
www.thegavel.net
Monthly newspaper about auctions

ORGANIZATIONS

American Society of Appraisers (ASA)
555 Herndon Parkway, Suite 125
Herndon, VA 20170
(703) 478-2228
www.appraisers.org
Organization with uniform criteria for professional appraisers

Gemological Institute of America (GIA)
5345 Armada Drive
Carlsbad, CA 92008
(760) 603-4000
www.gia.edu
Online and campus courses in jewelry designations. Online product catalog for jewelry
    instruments.

Hammered Aluminum Collectors Association (HACA)
P.O. Box 1346
Weatherford, TX 76086

(817) 594-4680
Publishes *The Aluminist* newsletter

International Society of Appraisers (ISA)
(206) 241-0359
www.isa-appraisers.org
Authorities in personal property appraising

National Auctioneers Association (NAA)
8880 Ballentine
Overland Park, KS 66214
(888) 541-8084
www.auctioneers.org
Members aspire to a code of ethics and professional standards
Also publishes a monthly magazine, *The Auctioneer*

A collector's club or organization exists for virtually every interest or hobby. Check the back of some of the price guide books, look through the antique newspapers, or search the Web.

WEB RESOURCES

Search Engines

www.dogpile.com
www.google.com
www.yahoo.com

Other Web Resources

www.artfact.com
Online database of antiques and art market, upcoming auctions and prices realized
By subscription

www.AskART.com
free search for artist and directories
and charge for member services

www.auctions.amazon.com

www.AuctionSniper.com
A company that automatically places your eBay bid for you

www.auctions.yahoo.com

www.barter.net
This company lists numerous Web sites of companies that barter

www.bbb.org
Better business bureau with reports about 2 million organizations on businesses and
   charities

www.collectors.com
Grading standards of coins, sports, autos, stamps, and music

www.collectors.org
National association of collectors and collecting clubs

www.eBay.com
World's leading online auction company

www.fleamarketguide.com
Guide for flea markets by states

www.garagesale.nearu.com
Garage sales across the country

www.irs.gov
Government tax forms and publications

www.[yourstate].gov
New York is www.nyc.gov
State forms for tax purposes

www.mapquest.com/directions
Free maps and driving destination directions

www.wnutting.com
Identification of Wallace Nutting furniture, prints, and look-a-likes

www.tourdekalb.com/yardsale
World's longest yard sale, held every August on Highway 127 from Covington, KY, to
   Gadsden, AL

www.vistaprint.com
Business cards, magnets, postcards, and brochures

www.warrensburggaragesale.com
Warrensburg, NY, world's largest garage sale, according to the *Guinness Book of World
   Records*
1,000 vendors townwide, first weekend in October

Web sites on specific collectible topics range from art to zithers. Do a search on
   your favorite search engine on the Web to track down further information on a
   specific topic.

Index

(Photo courtesy of www.TonyaMalay.com.)

About the Author

G. G. (Gwen) Carbone is a professional auctioneer, an eBay PowerSeller, an antique dealer, and a garage sale "junkie." With over 25 years experience, she conducts more than 200 auctions each year, including antique, estate, on-site, jewelry, and fund-raising auctions for civic and nonprofit organizations. Every week she entertains crowds of 500 or more and has worked with many celebrities, including *New York Times* best-selling author Wally Lamb (her high school creative writing teacher), Robin Williams, Julia Roberts, Bruce Willis, and Paul Newman.

Her quest for treasures has taken her to all 50 states and several other countries, including Canada, France, Wales, Scotland, and England. She is a lecturer and speaker on "Profitable Fund-Raising Auctions," "Bidding and Buying at Auctions for Newcomers," and "Searching the Planet for Garage Sale Treasures."

Ms. Carbone graduated magna cum laude from Eastern Connecticut State College with a bachelor's degree in English and a concentration in journalism. She is a graduate of the Certified Auctioneers Institute (CAI) and a member of the National Auctioneers Association (NAA). She is also a personal property appraiser and conducts real estate auctions throughout New England.

Her hobbies include fixing up and decorating her 14-room home with treasures she's found at garage sales, estate sales, thrift stores, and auctions. She stores her excess "junk" in her three-story, three-car detached garage. Ms. Carbone resides in New Hampshire with her husband, Chuck, and their two children. She would love to hear from you. Please contact her at trashtotreasure@mac.com or visit her Web site www.ggcarbone.com.

MY FAVORITE GARAGE OR YARD SALE
NEIGHBORHOODS

MY FAVORITE SHOPS